GHOSTS
IN
THE
VALLEY

By Adi-Kent Thomas Jeffrey

Acknowledgements

Grateful acknowledgement is here extended to former publishers of much of this ghostly lore: *The Sunday Magazine of the Philadelphia Bulletin*; *The Bucks County Courier-Times*; *Hiway Magazine*; *The Delaware Valley Advance*; *Bucks County Panorama Magazine*; and those three once-bright planets now below the horizon, *The Southampton Star*; *Bucks County Life Magazine*; and *Suburban Life North*.

As for the countless individuals and organizations who so ably and warmly assisted me in my researching, it is impossible to mention them all. I wish to sum up my appreciation to each and every one of them with a grateful "Thank you" for all their time and trouble in looking up sources, relating experiences, and answering numerous questions from this eager "ghost-chaser."

Published by
Hampton Publishing

Sixth Printing, 1991

Dedication

To my Gil who brought me to this valley and loves it as much as I.

Introduction

Ghost-chasing has been to me for many years the most absorbing, entertaining and rewarding activity I've ever undertaken. Not so much have I discovered this to be true from finding *where* ghosts are (though that they can be found still amazes me) but in finding *what* they are.

Explaining what ghosts are is a project all by itself. I won't go into that here, for this book is for entertainment, not for academic examination. That is the chief reason, as well, that where the incidents lend themselves to it, I have presented them with a story writer's technique so that you may experience for yourself what the subject experienced. The techniques I use may be those employed in fiction but these stories are not fictitious. They are all true and faithful in detail to the facts as I unearthed them.

Although I have chased ghosts all over our land, no area is more abundant with phantoms than the Delaware Valley. And in the Valley the colorful village of New Hope seems to be more than the gathering place of mere mortal artists and actors; it harbors a colony of apparitions, as well! You'll find them in close-formation towards the end of this book.

I sometimes wonder why so many desolate wanderers of the dark from the past and from the present—have flocked so readily to my side in this Valley. Probably because, like me, they think there couldn't be a better home anywhere!

At any rate, may they float and glide and scream and weep back and forth now across your path and may you meet them all and enjoy them as much as I have.

Table of Contents

The Bewhiskered Barmaid

In 1790 Old Lancaster Road was a gut-rutted, angle-changing route known as the Conestoga Trail along which lumbered the horse and wagon traffic of the day.

To accommodate the stream of peddlers, migrators, freighters, drovers and farmers, (as well as renegades, outlaws and smooth-talking hawkers) a string of taverns sprang up along the way, totaling a near dozen in the stretch from Philadelphia town to Paoli.

One of these swinging hostelries was the Blue Ball Tavern. Today it stands serene and beautiful and is a private home. In its early years it was anything but private and its owner anything but serene and beautiful. She was a hard-headed, two-fisted female shaped of an iron will and a whiskered chin.

Her name was Priscilla, commonly known as "Prissy." And Prissy had no equal among women. Inheriting Blue Ball from her father, Moses Moore, she ran it for many gutsy years as a tavern, handling the toughest of customers; barroom-brawlers that apparently left many a victim on the tavern floor or dead in his bed with his pockets clean.

Just how the murdered men met their various ends isn't clear, nor even if the enterprising Prissy herself had a hand in the deeds but dead on the premises they certainly were and that not just by legend. When a Philadelphia attorney, John Croasdale, bought the house in 1890 and had the workmen plant an orchard out back, the remains of several bodies were unearthed; a total of six skeletons in all.

Prissy had many problems. When times were bad due to the relocation of the railroad line and the subsequent loss of her main business, she changed the inn into a store, but that only after several fightin'-mad-run-ins with the railroad. Many a time she was out on the line shaking her fist and yelling threats to the crews as they chugged past. Another time when a train ran over one of her heifers and the railroad refused to reimburse her for it, she rendered the animal's fat and spread it on the uphill stretch of tracks.

In a short time she got her money.

Prissy lived a full century from 1777 to 1877. She saw the Civil War and her house used as a recruiting station for militia as well as an underground station for runaway slaves.

Prissy was married and widowed three times living out her final days alone and in as much a hub-bub as ever. Sporting by now a bristling fringe of white whiskers she was a fearful sight. The neighborhood children ran from her. Their parents, as well, looked upon Prissy with suspicion. Anyone passing

7

the old tavern on a dark and moonless night could hear strange noises clattering on the roof, they asserted. 'Twas the devil's split feet prancing, waiting for admission below!

What went on inside those thick stone walls for her salty century of life, no one can say for sure. But of what began to happen after her departure from earth, a great deal has been said and experienced.

Dr. Hannah Croasdale who teaches today at Dartmouth College was raised at Blue Ball. After her father had the dirt floor replaced with wood the family made the old kitchen into a library. Many a time Hannah sat in that mellow-aired room doing her home work. One evening when she was about thirteen and poring over her books in her accustomed place by the fireplace, she looked up and saw a figure standing on the step leading up from the library to the old "Commons Room." It was an elderly woman. She wore long full skirts and a big bonnet. She was slightly hunched over and from her chin shone a rim of snow-white hairs.

Impulsively, Hannah called out, "Hey! There's Prissy!" Before anyone else could see her, the figure vanished. The sight was not startling to the young girl, nor exactly a new experience for her. The Croasdales had been playing host to the old tavern-keeper for some time, or so it certainly seemed.

To this day, Dr. Croasdale recalls the many occasions when she and her mother would stop what they were doing and listen. Upstairs there would be a series of sounds. Over the library was an area that held two steps; then one. On these occasions, very distinctly, they'd hear footfalls overhead take the two steps; pause, then one.

There was also the instance of the "squeaking" bedpost. In the bedroom over the kitchen the Croasdales had a large four-posted bed. It was a favorite habit of Hannah's and many a person who wheeled around in the room quickly to grasp the bedpost and swirl past, the gripping hand making a s-q-e-a-k on the wood as he did so.

One day that slow bedpost "squealing" was heard so clearly below every-one felt certain someone had to be upstairs and swinging past that bedpost that very minute. Mrs. Croasdale made a quick run upstairs to check it out but there was no one there.

On other occasions, Hannah and her mother could hear the sound above of doors and dresser drawers opening and closing. When checked out, the room was always empty. Mrs. Croasdale and Hannah would just exchange glances and shrug. Prissy was a very determined woman and apparently wasn't thinking of lying quietly in any grave.

Perhaps the most sensational of Prissy's appearances was close to her last. That was in 1929. Hannah Croasdale recalls the circumstances very well. Down the road from Blue Ball and originally part of the inn property was an old smaller stone house. One day in 1929 it caught fire and burned down. It was big news in the area and the local village turned out to watch the firemen battle in vain. One neighbor brought a camera. He wanted to take a picture to send a former resident of that house.

There wasn't much left of the old structure but the remains of the stairway looked like a good shot. He focused his camera on the wall where the mark of the stair-treads could still be seen outlined in a zigzag pattern. Later, the photographer, the local paper and indeed the whole community were in a state of shock when the developed picture revealed a figure standing where the former steps had been. It was a hunched-over old woman dressed in long full skirts and a big bonnet. It was to everyone who saw it unmistakably Prissy!

So much agog was the community, investigators of every kind swarmed out to the charred remains of the old building and went over the stair wall with the keenest of eyes and most probing of fingers trying to ascertain if filtered light or shadows could have caused such an illusion. They couldn't find a single crack in the wall or any light angles whatever to explain the remarkable photo. To this day the incident remains one of the Main Line's most challenging mysteries.

Dr. Hannah Croasdale remembers the picture well. It was Prissy's last appearance she feels.

Or was it?

If you should ever talk to Howard Okie, Jr., you may conclude otherwise.

"We lived at Blue Ball in the early 1950's," Mr. Okie will tell you. "We had several strange experiences there. The principal ones involved the unexplainable opening and closing of doors. Particularly the door at the foot of the old stairway. We'd leave it open and find it closed or the other way around when no one had been near it nor was any draught present that could have caused it. The weirdest incident, however, occurred one evening as my wife and I were sitting at the dining room table, our dog, Clem at our feet. Now Clem was a Golden Retriever and they, as you know, are the most placid of animals. Yet that morning, Clem suddenly got up and tore over to the foot of the stairs where the door was open and growled and growled. His lips curled back, baring his teeth in near fury.

"I got up from my chair and talked to him, trying to calm him. He ignored me, continuing to growl ferociously and glare up the steps. Finally, his fierce growling grew louder and louder as he began to back up as though in retreat from some fearful thing coming nearer and nearer to him. I grabbed his collar, spoke firmly and reassuringly to him and looked up the stairs. I could see nothing. In the next few minutes the growling subsided and Clem slowly returned with me to the table.

"Though I saw not a thing, my wife and I always felt that Clem did. Some Thing that caused that dog's hairs literally to stand up at the back of his neck. He was retreating from some Thing that was threatening. We'll never know just what it was, but perhaps it was Prissy once again. Although she never meant to be, no doubt, she was a frightening figure. In her latter years the local village children—and even their parents—would go out of their way to avoid her. They were afraid her. Many thought her a witch in league with the devil!"

So ends the saga of Prissy, the lady with whiskers, one of the Delaware Valley's most unusual phantoms.

Shadows Over Sunbury

Overlooking the Neshaminy on Newportville Road just below Bristol, Pennsylvania, stands a regal house. She is fragile and beautiful as a Mardi Gras queen. Her white iron lacework facade frames her with the grace of a mantilla. The mansion has reigned at this wooded stretch of road since the early 1700's.

Her name has been recorded in history. Her walls have echoed to the footsteps of the great. Her picture has been sketched for books on Americana, reproduced in photographs and painted on china.

She is, indeed, immortal. Her name is "Sunbury."

But the least known side to Sunbury and the most interesting to lovers of the mysterious is not her history or her beauty. It is that which is the opposite of her sunny nomen—her shadowy side.

Let us walk up the lacy veranda, open the heavy oak door and enter the cool dark of the great front hall.

To the left is the dining room and beyond that the kitchen. Is there the sound of flying glasses; the shattering of dishes; the groan of chairs and tables being moved about? Blame it on the poltergeists of the mansion. They are the mischievous ghosts who have been making life irritating at Sunbury for some years. On one occasion they tugged the covers off the beds of the help as they slept—even tumbling the sleepy couple out of their beds.

To the right of the great hall is the parlor. To one side of the beautiful mantel there is hidden a secret compartment where, it is believed, valuables were tucked from raiders during the Revolution.

If the sound of chains rattling echoes through the quiet room, it makes its eerie way from depths far more hidden than the jewel cache. It comes from beneath the first floor from the inner recesses of the house where legend says a Hessian soldier once took refuge after escaping imprisonment. He met his end in the house and has haunted it ever since.

If we glance up the graceful stairway leading upwards from the great hall, we might see Sunbury's most charming ghost. She is a lovely lady dressed in a long white dress with a blue sash. She is most frequently seen standing at the top of the stairs. This intriguing creature haunted the mansion's mistress, Mrs. Alice Loring, from the time she was a child. Alice used to see her on many an occasion in her childhood home in Philadelphia.

"Who is the pretty lady visiting us?" she used to ask her mother.

10

"No one for you to be concerned about," her mother would answer with a knit of her brows and a quick pat on Alice's shoulder. It wasn't until Alice was grown that her mother explained that the lovely apparition who made her appearance from time to time was not a friend but a ghost.

"Ghosts don't haunt places," Alice told me, "they haunt people." And so it seems. The lady with the blue sash is proof. When Alice moved to the family homestead with her husband many years later, the white-gowned charmer moved with her.

Was that a low growl from the corner of the upstairs hall? And no animal there? Ah, but there is. See his misty form? Feel the soft furry form against your hand? He is Sunbury's most winning ghost—a gentle, curl-up-in-the-corner puppy who appears from time to time.

Now, we must not go a step farther. The pine-panelled bed chamber to our left down the hallway is supposedly shut off behind a locked door. But look, the door swings open. Lock it again. No avail. It will not stay locked. As the mistress of the mansion put it, that is her great Uncle Caleb's old room. Like its former occupant, it will not behave. Lock its door and it will become unlocked. Walk inside its hushed atmosphere and we will be assailed by the loud crying of a baby, first from this corner; then from that. Just shrug, as I shall do, as we walk out. We have been warned that crying like an infant is just one of Uncle Caleb's favorite haunting jests to make his intruder feel as disturbed as possible.

As we descend the stairway, what is that sudden draught that chills our backbones and whisks icily past us? Uncle Caleb, of course. Who else?

Down in the great hall again, we find opening the front door to the sunlight a welcome change. Before we can get outside a loud bombardment of knocking shakes the stately quiet. From door to door, upstairs and down, the knocking moves. Bang, bang, bang. On every panelled wall; every door; every sill and ledge the loud incessant knocking.

We nod. Uncle Caleb will be noticed!

Moving away from Sunbury down its curving lane, there is a sadness in leaving the lace-bedecked queen of Newportville Road. Her tableaux of ghostly scenes was a visit to another world.

Watch out! We must slow down as we approach the intersection of Newportville Road and Ford Road. The sun has set and the trees form a veil of darkness. Something shows up in our headlights. A man and a woman are standing in the middle of the road! They are dressed in the full skirt and the leather jerkin of the Revolutionary days.

Ah yes. Now it is remembered by us both. This is the spot we had been warned of earlier by Sunbury's owner. The ghosts of two horse thieves who were hanged at that corner centuries ago, haunt the place of their demise. More than one car has swerved at this gloomy spot to avoid hitting two walkers in the middle of the road. Collisions have occurred from time to time because of this ghostly pair.

We drive knowingly on. A perfect final brave touch for our visit to Sunbury, one of Pennsylvania's most haunted mansions.

Glassboro's Little Girl

The telephone was ringing upstairs. Vern Smith stepped out into the hallway at the foot of the stairs and listened to make sure. It was. Still he made no further move. He let it ring.

He hated to admit why. He had rented the old Victorian house on Main Street for a six week stretch while he was to be teaching at Glassboro State Teachers College in the summer drama department. He soon discovered the only phone in the place was on the second floor. This was proving to be a problem. Not because of the trouble in climbing the flight of steps but for a much more inexplicable reason. He dreaded that narrow, shadowy hallway with a fear he could almost bite on.

What made him feel that way? Childish, really. He hadn't been afraid of the dark since a little boy. Now he had to admit the moment he put one foot into that hall after dusk he became overwhelmed with real terror.

He stepped back into his bedroom now and slammed the door. He stood motionless until the phone stopped ringing and he could once more throw off a sense of guilt and go on about his business.

That night Vern Smith was awakened with a jabbing sense of annoyance. It was a moment before he realized what it was. It was the piercing sound of a child crying on and on, its breath spurting out hysterically between shrieks.

Where was it coming from? It was hard to tell. It certainly couldn't be from the second floor and there was only an empty attic above that. No one but he was in the house. It came from some house in the neighborhood, of course, but how loud the crying was to sweep across lawns and into his ears with such penetrating insistence.

Why didn't that mother, whoever she was, go to that child and bring the bitter crying to an end?

Vern lay there in the dark staring at the outlines of the window curtains billowing gently from a faint June breeze. When will that child stop crying, he wondered. The touch of pale moon glow kept him company as he lay there marking the time and waiting.

Hours must have passed before the wailing finally ceased. Thankfully, Vern turned over on his stomach and drifted off to sleep.

The next afternoon as Professor Vern Smith started up the walk to his house, he noticed a neighbor was out working on her lawn. Her children were playing beside her. Ah, thought Vern, an opportune moment to make a point!

He introduced himself to the lady. She chatted aimably then stared at him puzzled when the professor suddenly asked if any of her children was sick.

She shaded her eyes with one hand. "Why, no. What would make you ask that?"

Vern explained about the crying he'd heard most of the previous night.

"Well, I don't know who that could have been, but it most certainly was none of my children. I would have heard any of them and I did not. They are always good sleepers, and, too, it would really be impossible for you to hear them. Our house is too far away from you."

The neighbor paused a moment, then smiled up at the professor. "I know of one possible explanation. You are staying, I think, in a haunted house."

Vern raised one eyebow. "What makes you think so?"

"Well, before the present owner—Dr. Fritz Bell—your landlord, bought this place and the house was up for sale, a salesman came to my door. We chatted for a few moments, then he asked who was living in the old Victorian house. I told him that no one was but he said that was impossible as he'd just been there and had seen a little girl about eight or nine years old playing with her dolls on the floor. He'd been knocking for a long time and getting no answer. Yet he could see through the porch window that a child was in there. He expressed concern that the little girl should be all alone in the house.

"I told him there couldn't possibly be a child in there but we'd take a look to be sure. We made a thorough search of the place from the dirt cellar to the attic upstairs. Of course, we found no one. I'll never forget the salesman's face. He couldn't figure it out. I don't suppose he has to this day. Nor have I!"

The neighbor laughed softly as she finished speaking. The professor thanked her and went into his quiet Victorian house thoughtfully.

It wasn't exactly pleasant being the sole occupant of that lonely frame house that seemed bulging with shadowy corners, creaking floor boards and empty closets. But other than the usual groans from expanding woodwork and the scraping noises of tree branches against the porch roof at night, Vern Smith found the dark hours uneventful and he slept well.

For a few nights. Then one unbelievably hot night Smith tossed and turned in his bed close to the farthest wall. He got up and pushed it under the open porch window hoping to catch some little waft of summer breeze. Fitfully, he drifted off to sleep. But not for long. He was awakened by the sound of suppressed laughter.

He couldn't believe his ears. In the middle of the night just outside his house a group of children were playing games. He could hear distinctly their giggling as they were trying to be quiet but were too excited and having too much fun to be able to control their laughter.

Vern listened and decided they were playing "Hide and Seek." One was looking, calling out for clues; the others were hiding and trying desperately not to give themselves away.

What a ridiculous time to be out playing on the lawn. Surely, it must be those children again and once more, he'd have to talk to the neighbor. Yet, even as he was thinking that, his brain was telling him how foolish it was to believe any children could be out there running around in games after midnight.

Vern dropped back onto his pillow, cupped his hands over his ears and finally slipped off into sleep once more.

Again, he awoke sharply to the same giggling, now much louder and much closer to the porch. The sounds were just beyond the edge of the wood railing. Exasperated beyond measure at this point, Smith pulled himself out of bed, threw on a robe and grabbed a flashlight. Plunging out of the door he walked to the edge of the porch and flashed the beam in all directions. Nothing. He went down onto the lawn and walked all around the house. Somewhere, he was sure, strange as it might seem at 3:30 in the morning, there had to be some children playing out there on the grass!

He could find nothing but stretches of quiet green washed with a cool flow of moonlight.

Wearily, he plodded back to his bedroom and fell onto the sheets. What in the world was going on? His thoughts, dazed and confused, eventually blurred and fused into a fretful sleep.

He didn't know what time it was when he was awakened again. A distinct noise cut into his near-numb senses and he was driven awake; wide awake as though he'd never been unconscious for a second. Footsteps walking across the porch boards echoed into his ears. They were coming closer and closer towards the open window under which he lay!

Vern was lying on his stomach, his arms wrapped around his pillow. Realizing in a quick instant that someone was approaching the window over his bed, he suddenly froze, terror-stricken from his obvious vulnerability. He felt too paralyzed to move. He couldn't use a muscle or even think clearly in that instant of what he should do.

Before another thought could form in his brain, he felt a weight come down on top of him so heavy he thought it would press him right through the mattress and onto the floor! The force was powerful and immobilizing. His face was being pushed deeper and deeper into the depths of the soft pillow. Panic welled up inside him as it came to him if he couldn't get his breath in another minute he'd be dead!

Smith began pushing himself upwards as hard as he could against the pressure, using his arms with all the strength he could muster. The pain was intense but after what seemed endless seconds, he was able to get himself off the bed and onto his feet. He staggered to the wall switch and snapped it on. An empty room stared back at him.

Gasping and his heart beating wildly, Vern stood motionless for a while, studying every corner of the bedroom.

There wasn't a sign of anything different or of anything being disturbed.

Then something happened that sent his blood racing through his veins: he heard the quick patter of footsteps running off the porch!

In a spurt of determination to resolve the whole nightmare, he leaped towards the open porch window. Then he noted something as remarkable as anything that happened that long night: the window screen was still in place and untouched! Nothing could have possibly come into that room off the porch!

Despite the insufferable heat, Vern Smith pushed the bed back against the far wall. He collapsed on it in the most exhausted physical state he could ever recall experiencing in his life. He never again, for the remaining weeks of his stay, ever placed the bed under the porch window.

The days that followed that frightening night were torture for Professor Smith. He began to wonder if there were something wrong with him. Was he, for some unknown reason, losing touch with reality?

At the college that afternoon, he shared his experiences with his students. It had become unbearable to keep the strange incidents to himself any longer. Sharing brought him more comfort than he'd anticipated. He learned that many students who had boarded in that house the previous school year had been bothered by happenings as bizarre as his.

The stories poured out to him. Bob Murphy, for one, said that all of them, even an ex-Marine, heard frequently footsteps walking up and down the stairway. The sounds were always distinct, not just floor boards snapping in expansion or anything like that but a definite progressive slow creak one after another up or down the stair treads. One time in the middle of the night, Bob's roommate awoke him and asked him why he'd slapped him across the face! Bob hadn't. He'd been sound asleep. Their bedroom was the same one in which Professor Smith was at that time sleeping. Another boy said someone had tried to kneel on his back in the night.

Other students said they recalled hearing a child crying around three in the morning. Others mentioned the occasion when a guitar hanging on the wall below the stairs played in the middle of the night. One morning the instrument was found half way up the stairway. It could not have fallen off the deep-curved hook on which it had been hanging. It had to have been lifted off!

One of the most interesting occurrences in the house was told by a student who said that once while studying, his attention was caught by a moving figure nearby. He looked up just in time to catch sight of a little girl's pink skirt and the back of one patent leather shoe as she rounded the corner of his room and started down the cellar steps. He quickly followed after her, curious what a child was doing in the student house. He searched every nook and crook in the dark basement. There was no one there.

Later that afternoon the professor returned to his Victorian house a lot more at peace. Misery truly did find balm in company, he decided.

The following weeks passed uneventfully. Smith went away to visit friends for a brief few days—that was one peaceful and refreshing stretch—then he was back on the job, his mind filled with the work to be done on the forthcoming dramatic production.

The days and nights passed peacefully and Vern Smith was thankful for he knew the weeks ahead would be demanding. Already his responsibilities for readying the costumes, the sets, the lights and the publicity for the play had intensified and he found he was at the theater working into the late hours.

After quite a time of this, Vern felt he could not endure another taxing night of work. He left the theater early and went home to bed. He retired about a quarter to eleven and fell asleep almost immediately.

It could not have been long afterwards that he was startled awake by the most terrifying banging he'd ever heard. Not a loud crashing but a heavy, muffled thumping and it was happening on the other side of the wall next to him. The stairway was there, he realized in a second and some thing or some body was falling down it, striking each step with such force, the very wall was vibrating. He could hear the weight as it struck each riser, down, down, down with sickening thuds until it reached bottom.

Or did it? Vern listened, feeling as if his insides were turning over with the horror of it all.

No, the Thing didn't quite reach the bottom, nor would it cease. Just as he heard it descend, Thump! Thump! Thump!, he would hear the sounds commence all over again, starting at the top of the flight and falling downwards step by step.

Vern thought he was going to be sick. Over and over the ghastly sequence occurred and reoccurred.

Finally, he sat bolt upright and yelled at the top of his lungs, "Stop it! Stop it! Dammit! Stop it! Stop it!"

The thudding ceased. The trembling wall settled into sudden stillness. The air was thick with an oppressive quietness.

Dripping with perspiration, Smith fell back onto his pillow.

No passing truck; no storm; no high winds could his mind pick up to pass for an explanation. There was nothing in that deathly still night that could supply him with a solution. Like all the other weird happenings in that house, he was sure, the sound of a tragedy on those stairs was making itself felt again.

Somehow, Vern Smith got through the remaining weeks, although, how, he doesn't quite know, even to this day. It was a nightmare he experienced in that house that summer of 1967.

From those terrifying hours by that vibrating wall until almost the day of his departure, nothing further happened until the last night of his stay. That time he awoke for the final time within the walls of that sad house to the soft sound of a child's weeping. Very soft. This time he felt no fear.

"It's all right, little girl," he found himself saying out loud. "You'll be all right. And I won't forget you. You can be sure of that."

And he never has.

What is the story behind the haunted house of Glassboro? No one really knows. Students have held seances there and Ouija Board sessions on several occasions. All kinds of explanations have come forth from a child meeting a dire mishap to revelations of an underground passage and a concealed room. One psychic source came up with an actual name for the little girl. Elizabeth.

My investigations into the past of that house turned up only a happy family background. I could find no trace in actuality of a Civil War underground station or of any secret passageway or of any hidden room.

But one interesting fact I did unearth. A child in that house in the last century died at the age of nine. She lies buried today in a Glassboro cemetery. I located her simple gravestone. It read: "Elizabeth."

How dead is Elizabeth? After over a century, it would seem she still comes back. How did she die? No one living today knows that answer. If the very walls of the house are to be believed, she fell down that flight of steps.

But for those who believe in the psychic aspect of this world, it is nice to note, not all of the little girl's life was tragic. Perhaps, only the end here on earth. The rest, as with all other children, was filled with playing games or dressing dolls or running up and down the stairs or skipping across the front porch. Or even, maybe, just tucking into somebody's bed and holding hands with that individual.

I checked with the present owners, Michele and Barry Bitters. They nod knowingly at the question of a haunting child. A friend of their, Debbie Torrance, told them of a time she spent in that house. She awakened in bed about four in the morning. A cold feeling swept over her and she felt as though another presence were in the bed with her. In the next moment she felt a cool pressure slip into her hand. It was as if small fingers had slipped gently into hers, wanting to be held. After a second or two, the touch pulled away and was gone.

As for Michele and Barry, they, too, have a brief tale to add. Very early one foggy morning the couple awoke at the sound of a child's voice. Their bedroom was on the second floor. The voice came floating down to them from the attic overhead. It called, "Mommy! Mommy!" Then it was still. They have never been disturbed by anything since.

The last I heard, anyway.

One Man Show — the Ghost of Joseph Pickett

Many a renown artist has lived in New Hope, Bucks County's famous art colony and summer theater resort. But none has done the quaint and colorful town more proud, as the saying goes, than Joseph Pickett, the great primitive artist whose immortal "Manchester Valley" hangs in the Museum of Modern Art in New York City.

Pickett in his day, the late years of the last century and the early years of this, was the village grocer and butcher. He lived and ran his shop in a little brick house just off the canal on Mechanic Street. Some residents in the town still recall seeing his well-built figure hunched over some painting he was working on in between store hours. One of those paintings, few people realize, was drawn directly on the front brick wall of the building. There it still exists to this day under some thirty coats of paint unknown to the passer-by.

Also unknown to the average person idling by or even into the old house, the modest, big-handed, grey-haired Joseph still lives there. (The structure today harbors two shops: "The Cheshire Cat" and "Blackburn's Pasture".)

Oh, Joseph Pickett died in 1918 if you consult the encyclopedias but if you ask some of the many residents who have lived in that house since he was owner, you will learn quick enough that the unique Mr. Pickett still likes to hang around. Unrecognized in his life time, he most certainly is making up for lost acknowledgement in his "after-life." He seems to be bumping into or having good sport with scores of visitors in his old house.

Take Michael Majofski, for first instance. Mike lived in the Pickett House in the mid 1940's. He still vividly recalls being disturbed almost nightly by the pounding of heavy feet up a flight of steps on the side of the house. The noise itself was nerve-wracking enough but add to that the knowledge that the stairs no longer existed and you've really got the shakes, says Mike.

In the late 1940's the James Hoffmans moved in. In addition to James and his wife, Betty, there were two children, a three-year-old son and a baby girl. An incident occurred in that house to Mrs. Hoffman that she has never forgotten to this day.

Betty was working in an upstairs bedroom when she heard a sound of someone moving around in the master bedroom where the baby was asleep in a crib. She stopped what she was doing thoughtfully. What could that noise be? There was no one home but herself and the two children. Her son who was with her ran into the other room and called out, "A man is in here, Mommy!"

Betty Hoffman dashed into the room her breath tight in her throat. There sitting on her bed was a man. He wore dark trousers and a deep-toned shirt open at the neck. His hair was iron grey and he had a grey moustache. He said nothing but simply looked calmly up into Betty's eyes.

She spun on her heels and reached for the baby, snatching it quickly up into her arms as she made a grab for her son almost simultaneously. But in that second instant when she looked back at the bed, the man was gone.

With tense fingers she quickly put through a call to a neighbor. The friend hurried over and together the two went through every room. "I know an intruder was in here. Where did he go? How could he have gotten in?," were all thoughts racing through Betty Hoffman's mind. But nothing could be found. Not a sign of a person or a disturbance.

Finally the two women searched the outside where deep snow had packed an unbroken white covering all around the approach to the house. There were no footsteps but those of the neighbor's. "Eventually it dawned on me," says Betty Hoffman today, "I had seen Joseph Pickett!"

Not many years after the Hoffmans moved away, I spoke to the house's newest residents.

"Everything happens here," one of them told me. "At night we hear padded footfalls in the front room upstairs; or shutters banging even when there isn't a breeze stirring. Other times we've felt cool air flow past us like air stirring from someone's passing. We've found writing in chalk on the walls. Nothing that makes sense — just a hodge-podge of letters. On other occasions we've heard loud knocking on the back door. Always in the middle of the night. When I go down and open it, no one is ever there."

The other resident nodded her head and added, "Then there are the times I go down into the cellar for some canned goods or jarred foods. Many times a bottle of ketsup or a jar of cherries or olives will come flying directly at me off the shelf before I'm near enough to touch anything. We've also noticed the door to the artist's bedroom will not stay open. No matter how many times we open it, before too long has passed we'll hear a loud bang as it slams shut. Joseph simply wants to keep his door closed!"

Apparently Joseph still wants to do a lot of things. The present owners of the house, Howard and Linda Uible, who run the restaurant, "Number 8" across from the Pickett House on Mechanic Street, can tell you they've heard many things from the shop keepers there.

I found this to be true. The last two proprietors I spoke to on the canal side have heard footsteps on the inside stairs of the place when no one but themselves were present. And as for the owner of the "Cheshire Cat" and his assistant — well the stories of Joseph's mischief are manifold.

For example, Thomas Lynch will tell you, he leaves a bowl on a shelf in one room and finds it gone a few hours later. Then it will reappear the next day. In similar exasperating fashion other items in his shop move about or change places or vanish completely.

On another occasion he came in one morning to find the mortar between the old bricks of one inside wall fallen all over the floor on that side of the store as though someone had scraped loose the cement dust deliberately with his fingernails. It was a near-endless job to clean up the particles as well as get the gift items free of the grey-white coating.

One day, both Mr. Lynch and his assistant can tell you, a woman came into the shop to look around. When she got into the back room close to the area where the old stairs and entrance door had existed in Pickett's day, she felt a frightening icy feeling come over her. She fought off a shudder and went on around the store. As soon as she returned to that spot again, she felt a terrible sense of horror and revulsion. "Some one or some thing doesn't want me back there," she told the shop-keepers and hurried out. She's never been back.

Mr. Blackburn next door can tell you, also, of hearing footsteps on the stairs and bangings on the doors.

Recently I spoke with a woman who had resided in the Pickett House in the early 1960's. Had she experienced anything untoward there? Her answer was to the point.

"Why that old so-and-so used to lock the bathroom door on me! From the inside! So I couldn't get in! He'd push over that slip-lock bolt and the only way I could ever get it open was to send for the police!"

With such a wealth of mischief filling the old house by the canal, it's a wonder the historic "Manchester Valley" stays in place on the walls of the Museum of Modern Art in New York City!

Maybe it doesn't. I'll have to ask about that someday.

The George School Ghost

Thousands of quick-stepping bright-eyed students have been crossing and re-crossing the wide reaches of the George School campus in Newtown, Pennsylvania, for generations.

The scene is a familiar one to the countless number of people who have driven past the school on Route 413 since the earliest days.

But how many of these casual walkers and drivers have seen a little known corner of the George School campus . . . a recess hidden from the casual eye . . . the basement of the Revolutionary Tate House? And have seen it, not in the bland hours of daylight but in the heavy-lidded, heart-stopping blackness of midnight-time?

Warning: let only the heroes try it. And when the visit is made, carry the largest, stoutest candle that will burn the truest flame, for there will be the difficulty. When a certain spot on the basement floor is passed (beneath which a body lies buried, it is said) the candle flame will go out and the intruder will find himself alone in the damp darkness with only a thread of a shiver to recall that he is still alive.

Who lies in this restless chill-shrouded grave? The story goes back to the Revolutionary days. A Dr. James Tate inherited the handsome stone house from his father, Anthony Tate, who had purchased the tract in Newtown in 1756. Anthony died just a matter of months after the close of the Revolution in 1781 and the doctor took over as master.

Dr. Tate was an officer in the Continental army, serving as an army physician. Once the war was over, he could turn his attention to his first interest, the field of medical research. Finding a body upon which one could conduct experiments was a prime difficulty in those days. Many times guards were hired to watch over a tomb after a burial to guard it from desecration.

But Dr. Tate had a particularly favorable circumstance. A Hessian soldier, one of the prisoners kept at Newtown during the war, had died and was buried nearby. There had not ever been a soul to shed a tear, drop a spray of flowers nor care even to glance at the grave of this hireling from abroad. Here, then, was the doctor's built-in anatomy study waiting for him!

In the dead of night, he exhumed the forgotten Hessian and carried him into his laboratory room. Here he dissected the body under shroud of darkness with only the wan lights of tapers glistening over his hands as he worked.

When he was done he buried the soldier's remains in a shallow grave he hastily dug in the earthen floor of his basement. And he forgot the whole matter.

But the Hessian did not. The legend became a literally breathing one. For all the subsequent generations to follow, the experience of any visitor to the basement of the Tate House was the same. A lighted candle carried across the spot beneath which the soldier lay buried, would be abruptly blown out. In the black quiet of the night if one lay listening, one could hear booted feet tramping up the stairs from the cellar and go thumping along the upstairs halls.

In the year 1904 a prominent resident of Newtown, Mrs. Belle Van Sant wrote of this ghostly house ". . . it is a well authenticated fact that if you walk on the spot where he is buried with a lighted candle, the flame will immediately be extinguished."

What say the people who live in the Tate House today? Some years ago a reporter spoke to Mr. James Tempest, a mathematics teacher, who was a resident of the house at that time (today he is Assistant Headmaster of George School.) He nodded with interest at the story. He replied that there had been a puzzling mystery over the heater in the basement. The pilot light repeatedly went out. Several heaters had been tried and experts called in to examine the matter. There was no draught in the basement, no soot-clogged flue. Why the pilot flame went out had puzzled every examiner.

Later, a reporter visited the Tate House and spoke to a language instructor who lived on the second floor. Was there still a problem keeping a flame going in the basement heater?, she was asked.

"Someone comes frequently. You just missed the man who was here this morning to look at it," she replied.

Then she smiled. "Ghosts here?" She looked up and down the stairs and along the freshly-painted walls. "There are always creaks and scratchings and newly-made cracks in the walls. Perhaps the Hessian's spirit comes up from the basement and tries to get free from here, once and for all?"

Up the road a short distance stands "Sharon," the mansion built by Dr. Tate in 1804. It is an old colonial structure, once surrounded by a jungle of rare trees and shrubs. It was the showplace of Newtown in its day with glass for its windows brought from England. Its third story was a near-maze of dark closets that stretched under the eaves with doors leading on into other closets. There were also concealed doors entering the loft that extended over the back part of the home (a once-favorite haunting spot for bats and flying squirrels.)

Today, especially in the amber hours of early spring sunshine, the campus of George School looks warm and beautiful. The yellow paint on the Tate House and on "Sharon" join the bright air to welcome a fresh season.

But don't be deceived. The bright steps of students and the humming sounds of passing cars are only one side of the George School campus. There is a dark corner that will not be forgotten. The spot where legend says a Revolutionary Hessian soldier lies buried beneath the Tate House.

His breath, no matter how the new spring promises to waft, blows chill and deliberate deep down below. He will not allow the smallest light to penetrate his private tomb.

And don't try it. You will be no different from all the others.

The Ghost in Green Silk

It was a cool, brown-tinged evening in Bucks County, Pennsylvania, like many another in the fall of the year. Rad Miller put down his palette and brushes and looked out the window. It was too dark to paint any further.

The River Road outside the window of his two-century old house was quiet. His friend, Robert, was out and would not be back until later in the evening. It was an ideal moment for a rest before dinner.

Rad poked a listless fire into activity and stretched out on a sofa facing it. The little parlor was as still as a sleeping woods creature. There was just a whisper of a wind swishing around the attic windows above. Rad Miller sank his head down into the depths of a soft cushion and sighed. It was a peaceful hour. It was a peaceful village. He liked Lumberville and the river edge and the little white house which he had rented for a season. He was glad he had come. He closed his eyes. Sleep came easy in that listless time of the day.

The first sensation of the movement awoke Rad Miller with its coolness. It was the touch of an arm slipping gently under the back of his neck. His eyes opened. There was a strangeness to this awakening and he knew it instinctively even before his thoughts were coldly concrete.

In a second his head cleared. He was aware beyond the one sense of touch. The grey gauze of semi-consciousness was lifting. A beautiful young woman was sitting on the edge of the sofa beside him. One arm had curled behind his neck. The other laid in her full-skirted lap, camellia-white against the pale green watered-silk gown.

His artist's eye took in quickly the delicate face with its black penetrating eyes and the shining hair as smooth as polished onyx. Little jet twists of curls framed the soft curve of her neck. She was a beautiful young lady out of an ante-bellum era.

Rad Miller raised himself up slowly on one elbow. He opened his lips to say something. But nothing came out. The moment of grey gauze seemed to hover over his senses, binding his power to move or speak.

The oval face leaned over him. The beautiful young girl gazed hauntingly at him. The eyes were deep and troubled. Rad reached out to touch her. In that instant, she vanished.

The artist sat upright. Only the sharp hissing of the fire scissored into silence so thick he could almost feel its weight. He stood up and looked about him. There was nothing. He walked to the tiny stairway winding to the rooms upstairs. Nothing.

Later, when Robert slammed gaily in through the back door, he found a thoughtful friend staring into a dying fire. Miller told him the strange incident. Neither man could get it out of thought for the rest of the night.

For a few weeks, life in the little white house went on as normal. The visit of the young lady in mist-green watered-silk took on the air of a dream almost forgotten. The two artists went on with their work, unperturbed.

Then came an unforgettable evening again. Robert was out on an errand.

Rad had finished dinner and, as before, at the hour of dusk, lay down to rest on the fireside sofa. He lay quietly, his senses relaxed. There was no light in the room save the fire and a soft glow from two wall sconces flanking the French doors which faced him where he lay.

The kitchen door latch clicked open. Footfalls sounded from the kitchen, across the dining room floor, then paused at the entrance to the parlor where a step down existed. After a second's silence, the footsteps continued down the step and into the parlor.

His eyes still closed, Rad called out, "Forget something, Robert?" There was only silence. "Well?", Rad persisted.

Someone had come into the room. He knew it. Every sense told him so. At that instant a form passed in front of the soft lights from the wall sconces. Through closed lids, the artist saw the light black out as something passed between him and the glow from the wall lamps.

"Robert?", he called uneasily and opened his eyes.

The room was empty.

Not many days after this unnerving visit from the ghostly young lady, Rad was in the parlor again working on a dry point beside the French windows. He was intently leaning over the work, his crayon in hand when distinct footsteps sounded above him. They stalked disturbingly loud, crossing from one end of the room above to the other. Rad threw his crayon furiously up at the ceiling. "Get out!," he shouted, "Get out!". The footsteps ceased. Rad pushed back from his dry point and stalked upstairs into the darkness above. It was as though everything were covered in a black curtain. He snapped on lights as he plunged through each room. There was nothing to be found. All was quiet and undisturbed.

Robert began to raise questioning eyes at these tales. Why did they never occur when he was home? Then came that middle-of-the-night when Robert heard steps padding softly down the stairway to the dining room. He turned over in bed and listened. Rad must have gone down for a bite to eat. The next morning he asked the other artist why he was up in the night. Rad smiled. "I heard the footsteps, too, Robert. It wasn't I."

Robert shook his head, unbelieving.

Not long afterwards Rad Miller and his friend, Robert, left Lumberville and the white-eyed staring walls of the tiny River Road house.

Has the lovely lady in green watered-silk drifted away, too?

The present occupants of the house have never been disturbed by the silken footsteps of the young lady. But Rad iMller knew what he had seen and his friend, Robert, agreed with what had been heard.

One day a strange thing happened to Miller to give the perfect authoritaitve touch to his ghost mystery. He met an artist, Stanley, at a party one evening. They got to talking and each discovered that the other man had lived at one time in the little white house in Lumberville.

Stan nodded with fond recollections as he told Rad, "Yes, I bought that house years ago. In fact, I remodeled it. Interesting thing about that, you know. When I was crawling around the air space beneath the roof and ceiling of the upper story, I found an unusual thing to come upon in such a place—a pair of old handmade slippers, made of pale green watered-silk. With them was a silver mug. The mug had the remnants of a white substance in the bottom of it. Being curious, I had it analyzed by a chemist friend." Stanley shook his head before he went on, adding the final touch of wonder to a ghost story he had not yet heard.

"Know what it was? Arsenic."

Rad Miller thought back to that first brown-tinged evening. For years after he thought of it, especially on frosty firelighted twilights when the hours of dusk swept like gauze over a waiting thought. He later learned that many tenants, both before his occupancy and after heard the silken footfalls.

What has happened to the lovely young lady? Where is she today? The ghost in green silk, if she still walks, walks alone and unknown, her secret still measured in worth only by an old silver mug and a pair of green silk slippers.

Phantoms on the Third Floor

Five years ago when Jeannette Conti moved into the little apartment on the third floor of the old house in Norristown, Montgomery County, Pennsylvania, she experienced an almost indescribable feeling.

"I felt I was moving in where I didn't belong. That I was not the rightful resident but an intruder."

It was not long before manifestations began to take place that substantiated to her that deep-set intuition that someone else was present in that apartment with her.

"Once as I passed by the room that I use for storage but which had formerly constituted the bedroom, I felt a pocket of cold air envelop me. The rest of the apartment was warm but right in that room's doorway there was an icy chill. I checked but there were no open doors or windows to the outside or heater outlets that could have caused such a cold spot."

A short time after that incident as Jeannette was asleep in her sofa bed in the living room, she suddenly awoke with a sense of terror. Something was wrong! She opened her eyes to see a bright glow at the foot of the sofa.

Fire!, she thought and sprang to her feet with apprehension as she had not so very long before suffered great loss from a fire in her home.

When she took a good look there was nothing at the foot of the sofa. She clicked on a low lamp and looked slowly all about the room. There wasn't a sign of anything wrong. Yet, once more, she had that uneasy feeling of disturbance inside her; that feeling that she was living where someone resented it. That she didn't belong there and that some other person or persons did. Perhaps those who had lived before in that 150 year old house were hostile to the presence of anyone else beyond their own memories or spirits. Perhaps, to their way of thinking, she was a trespasser and they wished her gone.

Filled with these chilling thoughts, she looked into the dining room and saw the figure of a young girl standing there. She was completely sideways to Jeannette wearing an Empire style gown with a high bodice line and long full skirts. The girl's deep brunette hair fell straight to her slim shoulders. Her features were clear-cut as a pale cameo against the dark background of the grey room.

Before Jeannette could open her mouth and say something, the girl vanished.

On another occasion, Jeannette felt a presence with her again so strongly, she raised her head from her work and caught in the tail of her eye the form of an old man dressed in a black suit. She flicked a quick glance straight at him only to find he'd disappeared.

To add to her consternation, especially whenever she was upset or disturbed about something, a lamp on a small table in the living room would start flicking off and on. Off and on, it would go at least ten or fifteen times. In one instance this lamp seemed particularly erratic when a guest was visiting Jeannette. It blinked off and on constantly for a long while.

"I think someone besides myself is present in these rooms," Jeannette said to her, "and I think they don't like you and possibly think I am an intruder here also."

Shortly after that evening, Jeannette Conti made up her mind to something. She would speak to these presences there and "have it out" with them!

"Look!," she said, talking straight into the cool darkness of her apartment one night, "I live here now. I am alive. You are dead. You once lived here and wish to continue living here and I don't mind if you do. But I must stay here and live here also. So you welcome me and I'll welcome you and let's all live here together in peace!"

From that time on, Jeannette says she has felt only warmth and comfort in those rooms. "I've never felt uneasy since then. I no longer sense a strange unhappy presence. I no longer feel haunted by hostility. I feel friendly spirits live here with me and we all understand each other now. In fact, I feel these spirit-souls are company for me and a protection."

It has been several years now since Jeannette Conti came to terms with her haunters and all is complete harmony in the third floor apartment. All of which is no surprise to this Pennsylvania woman who has been sensitive to the World of the Sixth Sense since she was a little girl.

In various homes where she has lived or visited, Jeannette has experienced precognitive dreams; seen forms from a vanished era; felt actual physical pressure exerted against her to prevent her from entering a certain part of a house when no one was near her.

"I keep an open mind to such intuitions," she says, "and always will and so I guess they will keep coming to me. It has always been my wish to help other people. Perhaps, in sensing or receiving the presence of others, even those gone on to the next world, I am able to communicate with them and, as in the case of my Norristown apartment, live with them. So be it. I enjoy it."

Poltergeist in the Apartment

"Poltergeist" is a term used by believers in spiritism to define a certain type of ghost—a mischievous, annoying ghost. This spirit makes its presence known with certain phenomena which include, according to the *Columbia Encyclopedia*, "rapping, movement of furniture, the breaking of crockery for which there is no apparent scientific explanation."

There has been no better example of poltergeist presence than there was in the apartment of Carl Gualiardo in Lumberville, Pennsylvania.

Carl occupied a first floor apartment in an old frame house dating back prior to 1730. The structure, still there, is charming and beckoning. It stands on the River Road.

Inside the house is equally inviting. Carl's apartment stretched through three mellow rooms shaped of honey-toned plank flooring plus a sunny kitchen. The living room and dining room sheltered an old fireplace each.

What more could a tenant ask for? "Nothing," admits Carl Gualiardo who loved his river edge abode and cared for it like a doting parent. "But sometimes, one gets more than one asks for," adds this school-teacher. "I got ghosts."

A special brand of haunters, too, Carl has learned. Poltergeist. Annoying, bothersome spirits (if such they be) who needled him almost daily with tiny incidents. Small, but not too small to overlook.

He removed a shirt at night, placing it on the bedroom chair. In the morning it was gone. Where did he find it? On top of the refrigerator in the kitchen! He went to make coffee and found the top of the percolator missing. Hours later, having had to give up making coffee, he would find it under a pile of dishes in the sink when he knew vividly that when he had removed it from the percolator originally he had put it on the sideboard.

Then there was the minor annoyance of the telephone. Carl's handsome French-style telephone had tiny rubber feet that left a mark on the desk top, so he made a point to keep the phone in the identical spot on the desk in order not to mark up any further area of the wood surface. Almost every day when he came home from teaching the telephone would be in another place on the desk. Often so far out of position, the wire was stretched to its taut limits.

The desk chair also would be in a different position.

On another occasion, for no apparent reason, the towel rack in the bathroom fell from the wall to the floor.

Another time, a rapping came at the kitchen door at two o'clock in the morning. Carl got up and opened the door. There wasn't a sign of a person, an animal or a scraping tree branch. He has never been able to explain the incident.

One of the strangest occurrences happened one summer when during the heavy-rain-days a friend came in the back door, walked into the dining room and flopped down on a chair. At his feet on a newly cleaned rag rug, Carl saw with dismay a huge patch of heavy oozing mud. "Hey, look what you brought in on my clean rug!"

The friend apologized. "I'll get someone in tomorrow to clean it for you, don't worry."

That night when Carl returned home he made a point to take a look at the rug to see how badly the mud had set in. The rug was perfectly clean. There wasn't a sign of the mud patch, nor even the remains of a stain. It was utterly clean.

He called his friend. Had he sent someone over while Carl was out? Of course not. Take a look again. Must be the darkness deceiving him. By sunlight the next morning, the friend assured Carl, he'd see the mud again. But he didn't. The next day the rug looked as spic and span as it had the night before.

Added to the confounding incident was a still more remarkable rug phenomena. In the living room Carl had a 9 x 12 Oriental rug which stretched before the fireplace area. Through the early spring months, right after moving in, Carl had walked across it in his bare feet every day. Then a strange thing happened. One morning he walked across it and stepped into a sopping wet corner. He looked down. The near corner of the Oriental rug was dark with wetness. He reached down and felt it. His hand came up so moist, tiny drops fell from his finger tips.

He could scarcely believe it. From where could such a quantity of water in the middle of the living room come? He examined the fireplace chimney; the windows (which were painted shut and never opened); the cellar beneath the parlor to see if any pipes or vents exuded water from beneath. Nothing. No cats or dogs had ever come in. Nothing was open nor leaking from the ceiling. It could come from nowhere. Yet the rug corner was wringing wet day after day. In spite of repeated attempts to dry it out before the fire, the corner of the rug remained soaking wet for two months (even though the floor boards beneath were completely dry).

Finally the rug began to smell of mold and Carl, in late August, took it up and disposed of it.

These phenomena were not partial to Carl. They occurred also to friends. Take one Labor Day weekend when friends came for a visit. Carl told them of his poltergeist. The two men laughed, "Who you trying to kid?"

But they didn't laugh for long. Just before retiring one put down a book he was reading and removed his glasses. The other came into the room just as his friend was fumbling to set his glasses down on the night table. The incoming friend reached for them and set them down on the table for him, next to the book, then turned the light out.

In the morning the friend couldn't find his glasses. "I put 'em right there next to your book," said his companion. He stared. There were no glasses. They began to look about, under the beds, under the table. Where did they find them? On the coffee table in the living room. The friends stared at Carl when he came into the parlor. "How can that be? We didn't leave our room last night!"

How can it be? What caused the disturbances of every nature in the apartment? Believers in spiritualism say that it was poltergeist, mischievous spirits. Parapsychologists studying such phenomena believe them to be the result of psychic powers in the thoughts of those living now in the house which are in rapport with the thoughts and experiences of those who lived in the house before them. The actual movement and displacement of objects is due, say the parapsychologists, to psychokinesis, the science of the control of mind over matter. The thoughts of the occupant of the home, unconsciously, cause the movement of the furniture, dishes, phones, etc. And the thoughts of the present dwelling subconscious could conceivably be touched by the thoughts of the subconscious of the former occupants.

Who lived in the house before Carl Gualiardo? A couple of unusual background. She was educated in India; he in Hong Kong. Their apartment radiated Oriental influence in cobra snake candlesticks; Chinese lanterns; Oriental rugs.

They were an unhappy pair. They were said to feel at odds with the world; with the country; with their town; with each other. They died under identical circumstances in their middle years . . . only six months apart of a stroke which occurred on the very sofa which still stood in the parlor.

Did their chip-on-the-shoulder attitude towards life touch the life of Carl Gualiardo? Through their thoughts still suspended in the mellow rooms of the old house or through their restless unhappy spirits come back to haunt their successor in the house? The objects involved in the weird incidents except for the rag rug did belong to that couple.

There are not answers, only ideas Carl Gualiardo ponders. Will he ever again come home and find mud on the rug or his phone displaced or chairs moved? He thinks often of that possibility.

The Haunted House of Centennial Row

It was built in 1876, the year of Philadelphia's Centennial celebration of our nation's independence. It was one of a block of houses, each a structural testament to the crystal-chandeliered cream of Philadelphia society. The distinguished stretch of handsome homes along the great wide Broad Street of Philadelphia came to be known as "Centennial Row."

This particular house defies time, tailoring and tenants. Unlike its Centennial neighbors, it will not behave like a home, an office or a store in this world of today. It stands as a rebel. An irascible, touchy, stiff-necked gentleman-of-the-old-school who will not stand for any label, license or landlord.

This one house has been for sale or for rent for years at a time. It has had fresh paint; it has had a modern store-front superimposed on the old structure to change its mien. It has had new and various tenants over the years but none for long.

Why?

Ask a man who lives fairly far from Centennial Row today in Jenkintown, Pennsylvania. His name is Thom Street. He is well-known for his skills in art restoration. He is also an excellent professional musician. But on the subject of ghosts Thom turns his attention away from art and music and discourses happily on the wonders of psychic phenomena. Once in that realm, Thom is also once again in the house in question, the Haunted House of Centennial Row.

Thom was a close friend of the owner of that home in the 1930's. When he tells his story today, out of respect for the privacy of the elderly lady's family whose name is still prominent in Philadelphia social circles, he refers to the one-time mistress of the home as Miss Knapp.

The snowy-haired and gracious Miss Knapp, recalls Thom, spent a long life of happiness in her Centennial Row house . . . until the death of her father. From that time on, the polished mahogany, the silver tureens and the gilded sconces were no longer a pleasure. Loneliness, uneased by quivering gas lights, lurked in every dark corner of the house.

Miss Knapp decided to move. Thom offered his assistance. He and a close friend agreed to undertake the onus of packing up the household goods. Miss Knapp gratefully accepted.

On the day she made ready to depart and was putting her sole key to the front door into Thom's hand, she noticed the two men staring up at a carved Victorian hat rack which loomed over the front hall just inside the entrance way. A man's hat was hanging on one of the brass hooks.

Thom recalls how Miss Knapp smiled sadly at that moment and explained, "That was my father's hat. He always kept it there. After he was gone, I just couldn't move it. I thought it should stay right where he'd left it."

Thom and his friend nodded sympathetically but when they let themselves in the next morning ready to go to work, Thom went straight to the hat rack. "Before we start anything, let's dispose of this." He plucked the hat off the hook and marched down to the hall closet under the stairs, opened the door and threw the hat up on the shelf.

After a full day of sorting and packing boxes downstairs, the two men left. Thom closed the heavy front door after him and locked it securely, testing it to be sure.

The next morning the two friends met in front of the house. Thom opened the door. It took a moment to adjust to the dimness in the hallway. When they did, the two stared at the hat rack and then, increduously, at each other.

On the brass hook of the carved hat rack hung the old felt hat.

Once again, Thom took it down and placed it carefully on the hall closet shelf. As he walked back towards his friend, he shook his head. "Unbelievable. I thought I put that doggoned hat up there yesterday! I must have been dreaming."

The other man scratched one ear as he said, "I thought I saw you put it up there, too!"

The two men forgot the incident as they busied themselves gathering up household effects and packing them in crates and barrels. As soon as twilight fell, the wisps of gas heat and the trembling gas jets from the walls were too faint and too eerie. The men called it a day and departed.

The next morning upon entering the hallway both men let out low gasps. The old hat hung at its accustomed place on the brass hook. The two friends turned and stared at each other. Slowly, Thom took the hat down and carried it once again to the closet shelf.

"Someone's playing a weird game," he said, thoughtfully. "But how could that be? I've got the only key to the place there is!"

The same incident repeated itself for the rest of the week. Neither man could explain what was happening but by that day, neither wanted to experience it again.

"We're getting the job finished today," announced Thom as the two made their way to the dining room at the rear of the house. As the friend started packing crystal vases and china plates into straw padding, Thom offered to start bringing the packed boxes down from the library overhead.

"I know of an easy way to do it," said Thom. "There's a tiny stairway that rises between the walls down here and leads to the library above. Let's see if we can use it."

The two men felt with their hands around the walls until Thom found a narrow door on the far wall. As he opened the door with a creak, a dust-coated staircase opened to their eyes. It was musty and criss-crossed with cobwebs. "Doesn't look as though it'd been used in a century," observed the friend.

Thom nodded as he squeezed himself into the small passage. "Too small to pull crates through," he murmured woefully. "Oh well, I'll just use the regular stairs." Thom pushed the slim door shut until it blended once again with the elaborate wall paper design and disappeared to the sight. The catch clicked as the hinges groaned, creaked and slipped into silence.

Hours later the two friends sealed the last carton in the dining room. They had worked later than usual to finish the job. Now the air in the dining room had the chill of a tomb. The light was impossibly faint as it was long past dusk. The gas jets gave off only a whimper of light. From the old cast iron heater in the center of the room mere flickers of red light through the decorative holes pierced the gloom.

Suddenly the two men faced each other. There was unexplainable tenseness in the room. A cool air fanned against their faces as though somebody were walking past them and at the same time the sound of soft footfalls padded gently by them and out into the hall. The men were stunned into immobility. From the corner of their eyes they both saw simultaneously the little doorway to the secret staircase was standing wide open.

Thom swallowed hard. "I shut it tight!"

"I know you did. I watched you. But it sure isn't tight now!" The friend stared at Thom with eyes wide open.

The men set to work like automatons dragging the last of the cartons to the front hall.

"I'll call Miss Knapp in the morning and tell her everything's ready to go. The movers can pick up the crates tomorrow." Thom swung about and took a final check-out look down the hallway. "Let's go!"

As Thom reached up to extinguish the last gas light by the front door, he hesitated a second. On the hat rack hung the old felt hat.

"He must have come out to say 'goodbye' to us, knowing we'd be leaving for good tonight," murmured the friend.

Thom reached up again and turned off the jet. As he closed the heavy door and locked it for the last time against the darkness of the great house now unlived and unloved, he nodded his head in agreement.

"And I don't plan ever to return," added Thom.

He never has.

The rebel house still stands overlooking Broad Street. It has defied so many would-be tenants and varied disguises. Does anything still disturb the darkness of night behind those old walls?

Miss Knapp has long since been gone. Only ghosts, perhaps, can supply the answer to the mystery of the Haunted House of Centennial Row. And they aren't talking.

Or are they?

The Schoolmaster of Dark Hollow

In Warwick Township of Bucks County exists one of the most rugged and naturally beautiful areas in all of the Valley. Several roads which can be reached from Route 232 as it makes it way through Richboro and on up towards New Hope take you down into this valley of enchantment.

Watch out though! The spell woven there is born of a haunting, unforgettable past. This area lives up to its foreboding name—Dark Hollow.

As you cross the steel bridge spanning the stream in this mysterious valley, stop a moment.

Do you hear the whistling of a fisherman as he passes by with dreams of bass in his head? Ah, he is indeed a dreamer if legend be ruler in this kingdom of shade. It is said no fish, no live thing comes from this wandering stream ever since the darkest days of the hollow's past.

Once right where the present day bridge holds you up over a listless brook, stood a bridge of worn timbers. Many times it rumbled to the hurried steps of some woods-walker who found himself out too long and too late with the shadows of this glen. Scarcely a wanderer of the woods came and went in the days of the 1800's, whose heart did not beat faster with every twig-snap underfoot.

Yes, Dark Hollow was indeed dark. There were no homes within its gloom at that time. The only sign of any former civilization was the remains of an old schoolhouse. The broken structure of moss-covered stones stacked beside the shivering waters of Dark Hollow Run, seemed to groan as the winds sifted through the crevices and cracks.

Passersby were drawn irresistibly towards this ruin to hear the ghostly mutterings, but none stayed long. The scratchy arms 'of dead trees caught hair or a disturbed owl split the silence of the woods hollow with a screech.

Dark Hollow became known as a glen of ghosts.

What lay behind the deserted schoolhouse filled only with moss and spider webs and, according to some of the more daring probers of the day, with blood-freezing wails?

It all began in the very early years of the last century. A Yankee schoolmaster, hard as the rocks of the New England coast which bred him, was hired to conduct the school in this spruce-thick valley. His discipline was as harsh as his flint face. He was tall and thin and seemed to hold onto his punishing rod as though such contact supplied him with the very breath of life. He used the rod more frequently than the multiplication tables in that schoolroom. The children dragged with dread to school each day. Most returned home with bruised bodies, thrashed knuckles and frightened eyes.

One day when the schoolmaster was in full measure of ire, he wore out his switch on the children's backs before the day had scarcely gotten under way. He decided he must get a stouter rod with which to teach his lessons. He stalked out into the woods.

Without a moment's delay, with scarcely a glance at each other, the pupils arose and fled. Once home, each spilled out a breathless tale of horror and firmly refused to return. Not a parent demurred. The children were to be disciplined, but not terrorized. A meeting was planned to discuss further action. Meanwhile the children were kept home.

The schoolmaster returned, swinging the switch with anticipation. When he stepped into the empty room his face stared in white fury. They would return, he told himself. He had disciplined each child to know he must be obedient. Each would return.

Soon he received word. He was dismissed.

Impossible!

But he was asked to leave. The schoolhouse was closed down. This was the end for the Yankee man with the bony frame and the cracking switch.

Months went by. No-one ever saw hat, coattail nor rod of the man again. The whole town sighed with relief. Gradually the pupils buzzed excitingly again of their harrowing days in the cold stone schoolhouse in the woods.

One day, a former pupil decided to walk through the glen and have a peek at the old room. A broken shutter was banging in the late winter wind. He pulled himself up on tiptoes and glanced into a shadowy interior. His breath caught in his throat. There in the dim light was a grey form, a near-shapeless mist, but distinct in identity. It was the gaunt figure of the schoolmaster, sitting at his desk. He sat with rod in hand and eyes focused on the door, waiting for his pupils to return.

The boy thrust himself away from the window and fled through the crunching dryness of the glen. The story he told spread far and wide through Bucks County. It was remembered for decades afterwards. Many more tales followed of the ghostly school master awaiting the return of his class.

Today memories of this tale have fallen away from the minds of this generation. The stones of the old schoolhouse are not even to be found. But listen! As you step off the bridge and start up the winding hillside road shadowed with the thickness of trees, do you hear the story again? Told in the crawling touch of tightening twigs? Wailed in the winds? Recalled in the stale scents of forgotten ferns and lifeless leaves?

You will leave Dark Hollow. But you will never forget it.

Lambertville's Lady with the Lute

John Warford lay half-awake in his bed as the grandfather clock in the living room below chimed three times. When the last note had settled into silence the house about him seemed like a deserted mansion in a Gothic novel.

He loved the old Lambertville house, the handsomest in all of New Jersey, he felt. Yet he'd not been in it long enough, he felt sometimes, to put his own presence in there. It always seemed filled with the past of another era. Perhaps of another person. It was a feeling he often had about the place and it would well up persistently late at night in the depths of darkness and quiet.

He sighed and tried to relax. It had been a long day at his florist shop, the Flower Box, and he'd had scores of orders to fill plus the work he was ever squeezing in to get his new home settled. Having just recently bought the 1812 brick and stone house he was now putting in longer hours than ever restoring the place to its original decor and Directoire period of furnishings.

John closed his eyes, more thoughts pouring into his night musings. He pictured to himself the long wine-red draperies he'd just hung at the floor-to-ceiling windows. Their heavy folds drawn back with gold braid, they seemed right out of a Napoleonic palace. Nice. He liked them. And the oil paintings and the Chippendale chairs — everything would be completely authentic right from the Waterford crystal chandelier in the dining room to the rosewood tea caddy on the black marble mantel in the drawing room.

He smiled to himself. George was a lucky charm at finding just the right pieces for that Empire period house. His good friend, George Rainforth. It was he, in fact, who'd snared the rich wine draperies from a hotel auction not so long ago.

John wondered to himself now in the semi-darkness was the lovely house becoming an obsession? If so, what a wonderful obsession! Loving history and the place's colorful historical background — one of the village's earliest settlers and a close friend of George Washington had built it — there could be no other dedication, outside of his nearby flower shop, that could interest him more.

John's eyes snapped open. Something had interrupted the flow of his late-night thoughts. A soft pressure near his blanketed feet caught his attention. Someone, very gently, had sat down at the foot of his bed!

He lifted his head from his pillow hesitantly. In the diffused light that floated from the hallway into the room through the door transom, he saw a figure seated at the end of his bed. It was a young girl dressed in a silky mist-blue gown of the Napoleonic period. In her hands she held a lute. In the next second her milk-pale fingers were plucking softly away at the instrument's strings. He could hardly believe his ears. In the semi-darkness he was listening to the quaint strains of an old tune from the distant past.

The girl's eyes kept their gaze at the strings as she plucked and swayed slightly with the rhythm of the song. After a few minutes she was finished.

She lay her slim fingers across the strings to settle them to silence and looked over at John.

He pulled himself up to a near-sitting position and started to speak. In that instant she vanished from sight. He was alone in the dusky bedroom again.

It was an experience that crowded John's every waking and sleeping thought for weeks. It was such a strange incident and yet, in its own out-of-this-world way, so right for that house. Somehow the young lady semed to belong there. Perhaps, more than he who now owned the place.

Less than a month after the old occurrences, John came home late at night again and was busy putting some clothes away in the closet of his dressing room across the hall from the bedroom when once more he felt that he was not alone in that house. Something made him turn away from the closet and peer across the hall.

There she was. Her slim form stood erect in the hall's dim light. Her blue-mist gown fell in delicate lines from the high bust-line straight to the floor. The folds were still shimmering with movement as though she had just reached where she was. The lute was resting quietly at her side, held in one hand. She gazed intently at John for a quick moment; then she was gone. There was nothing in the hallway now but the low glow of the antique bronze lamp.

That was about a year ago. The lovely lady with the lute has never returned again. Perhaps, suggests John, because she has satisfied herself that the house is in good hands and will be cared for and loved as it was when she lived there.

No other explanation can John Warford supply for the strange visions. But he can add one interesting fact that may or may not have a bearing on his ghostly experience. As a child, John lived in Lambertville and took music lessons in that very house. He always had a love of the early 19th century which the old place exuded even in those days. Buying the house eventually was like a dream of long years come true.

Does the lovely lady of the lute bring into his presence in a heart-touching way all the past of music and beauty he loved within those walls?

Was she also a student there many, many years ago? Is that their bond, though a century and a half apart? (The house was, during the last century, a girls' school).

Explanations, feels John, for such experiences are not easily come by.

Ghosts in a Gift Shop

Near the intersection of Route 232 and Almshouse Road in Richboro, Pennsylvania, stands the home of John and Margaret Gallagher.

It is a house that commands attention. It belongs to a large and busy family in which the husband and wife and five children work together to shape a future which destiny forced upon them when an automobile accident injured the breadwinner. The home harbors a shop of candles, candies and gifts. So the house is more than a home, it is a business and a family enterprise.

The house has the importance of age. It was owned by one of the early settlers of Richboro.

The old Richboro home draws attention for more cause than these earthly ones, however. It houses the noisy, running, restless ghosts of children. Ask any of the Gallaghers who live there and almost each has had his own disquieting experience. They all agree on each disturbance: it is some manifestation of the presence of a child or several children.

It all began a few years ago when the Gallaghers were just getting a foothold on the work to be done in settling down in an old house. The eldest-daughter, Kathy, and her young husband were preparing for bed when a strange thing happened for that late hour of the night. Kathy stopped winding her hair on rollers and looked at her husband. He put down a shoe and listened. Underneath their window children were crying.

What were children doing outside at midnight? It was obviously the fretful crying of young children. Were they lost? Were they alone?

The crying got more persistent, more alarming. Both Kathy and her husband leaned out the bedroom window and looked down below. The crying stopped instantly. There was nothing there but an empty street, cold and disinterested in the light of a pale moon.

Surprised, the two went to bed. By the next morning the weird incident seemed like a dream. Yet each knew it was not. It remained a curious event that neither could explain. To be sure that it was not without solution, Kathy questioned the neighbors next door. Did they have children or know of any near by? They did not.

Several months later, Margaret and John Gallagher had put the little ones to bed, did a few chores in the house and, finally, a little before the clock struck twelve, made their weary way up to bed. Margaret was just starting to brush her hair when her hand froze. A child was running through the house below. The Gallaghers stared at each other.

Margaret sat with her breath caught for a surprised instant. In the stillness of the dead-of-night house, the quick thumping footsteps were startling. They were heavy. A boy's, quite positively. The heel came down hard with each rapid step. How could it possibly be Tommy or Eugene?

She arose. John followed her into the hall. If it were one of the boys, he'd have to discipline him. But the question was already there, before they checked the boys' room. They both knew in the back of their bewilderment that it was not one of their sons. They just knew it was not their running steps.

They were right. It was not. Tommy and Eugene were fast asleep. Margaret and John edged slowly down the stairs. The steps creaked under the weight of each foot fall. The running pattern pounded into the living room beneath and ceased. John turned on the lights in the old parlor . . . and the dining room. They were empty. There wasn't a sound but the ticking of the **clock.**

It was not many months after the running-steps incident that the ghost children came again. This time to John Gallagher alone. He was reading late one night in the old parlor. Margaret had gone upstairs and was preparing for bed. It was a night John felt unusually well. It was one of those rare nights he felt he could relax with a good book. The children had long been asleep and the house was a haven of quiet. A unique moment in a household of four young children!

John turned a page. In the dense stillness of the night, the soft rattle of the paper page was like a momentous sound. He read quietly on. Margaret called down "goodnight" and turned in. The house was dark save for the yellow glow of the lamp where John read.

It all began delicately, at first. So gently and naturally, John was hardly aware that he was hearing anything. Then gradually his senses became aware he was listening to the voices of little children. The tones were light, tuneless, the lisping ramblings of the very, very young. One moment the tinkling notes were those of laughter, then chattering back and forth between several voices. In the next instant, the tripping notes were slipping up and down the scales in a light singing. It seemed a group of two and three year olders were holding a midnight conclave above!

John got up and moved quickly up the stairs. He knew without looking, it was not his own children. He found what he knew he would find. The upstairs was absolutely quiet. Everyone was asleep. The air was dense silence. Nothing more.

To this day, years since the first manifestations, the Gallaghers have lived with these curious and disquieting ghostly children. Who are they? Why are they there? The answer is always in the past . . . perhaps, tied with a link to the present.

Did some family of many children live there in the long ago? Did a tragedy strike their father? Their income? Their homestead? Did the mother of some centuries-old household listen to the plaintive weeping of her young children as she packed all their worldly goods and moved away? Did the very little ones play to the last moment in their tiny nursery above, serving tea to passive china-faced dolls?

Did some young son chase through the parlor searching for his dog? Was he playing one last game of tag?

Was there a pale-mooned night at some later time when the children came back and stood outside the house, crying for the warm walls that housed them no more?

Who are the children? Do they come back to share the little moments of joys and sorrows experienced by the large Gallagher family living within those walls? Can destinies and understandings be shared by thoughts centuries apart?

Some questions in life can never be answered, only pondered. Questions which hover in every corner of the old Richboro house. Thoughts that may forever remain with the Gallaghers.

The Hostess with the Mostest Ghostes

If, as Alice Loring put it in my talk with her about her family manifestations (see "Shadows Over Sunbury"), ghosts haunt people and not houses, then surely a hospitable lady in northern Pennsylvania should get the Apparition Award. He name is Hilda Chance and in nearly every home she's lived in, specters have paid her visits.

Such ghostly goings-on have occurred to her in one house after another in the Delaware Valley area.

Years ago one of the eeriest incidents happened in her girlhood home in Harrington, Delaware. Hilda's mother awoke early one morning as her husband lay peacefully sleeping beside her, when she heard the catch of the bedroom door click open and some one walk in.

She could hardly believe what she saw. It was the figure of her husband coming into the room. He was carrying a suitcase.

Quickly she glanced over at the form beside her. Her husband was obviously there and deep asleep. She didn't close her eyes again but lay there thinking and wondering what the phantasm of her spouse could mean.

"Where are you planning to take a trip?," she asked her husband later at breakfast.

"I'm not planning to take a trip anywhere," he replied with an amazed expression. "What would ever make you think I was?"

Hilda's mother shrugged and put down her coffee cup. "Just think you're going to, that's all."

She was right. Before very long, her husband did take a trip. She saw him return carrying the suitcase, just as she had seen him in her early morning vision. Not long after his return he died.

After Hilda was married and had a family she lived in a home in Boothwyn in Delaware County, Pennsylvania, which she and her husband, Joseph, rented for the years their children were growing up. "We had only one visitor there," relates Mrs. Chance, "a little boy."

It seems a young child would appear to the Chance children whenever they were sick. While the family was feeling fit and fine, all was quiet (psychically, at least); then the moment one of them would feel ill, he would report a visit from this strange little boy.

"He would talk to my children at such times and the message was always the same: 'Leave this house with me! Come on! Run away; Follow me and I will show you a nice place. A much nicer place than this!' I don't think his appearance frightened them so much as it aroused their curiosity. They began to wonder who he was and where this 'nice place' was."

Crackling along in her matter-of-fact voice, Hilda Chance tells how she felt sure that the young visitor was the spirit of some child who had lived—and perhaps died—in that house. He wanted the company of children near his own age, she was sure, and that was why he was always showing up at their bedsides and not hers and trying to persuade them to follow him into the "spirit world."

She looked into the past history of that Boothwyn home and unearthed the fact that some years before a little boy had died there of meningitis. His physical description tallied with that given by her children.

Some time later the Chances bought a home. It was a large old stone mansion ("gracious," Mrs. Chance describes it) surrounded by beautifully-planted grounds. The house and property had once belonged to a locally-prominent family who owned the manse and a great deal of acreage there in Upper Chichester County in Pennsylvania.

"When I would be alone in that house, working or reading or writing downstairs," says Mrs. Chance, "I would hear what sounded like the footsteps of a little old lady padding about on the second floor. I would hear much opening and closing of doors and closets and the creaking and slamming of dresser drawers as though they were being opened and closed one after another. I would stop and listen attentively. It was always easy to picture the little old lady cleaning house and putting things away. I could hear the hustling of her busy feet for hours at a time. One day I decided to try to meet this friendly spirit whom I felt undoubtedly was the former mistress of that house. I went to the foot of the stairs (oh, those beautiful old curved banisters) and called up, 'Welcome to my home now! Come on down and let's have a friendly visit!' Abruptly, the sounds ceased and I never heard them again.

"After that, though, we all became badgered with other strange occurrences. Loud knocks banged over and over on different doors when no one was near them. Thumps would trounce against window panes close to where we were sitting. Each time we'd investigate we'd find no one was near and there could be no cause for such disturbances.

"But oddest of all such annoying manifestations was the disappearance of various articles. Things actually vanished from sight right alongside of where we would be sitting! Just there one minute and gone the next! Sometimes, never to be found again."

Years later, the Chances moved away from Upper Chichester to retire in an old farmhouse in northern Pennsylvania where they reside today—and are still playing host to ghostly visitants.

"One night," Hilda Chance related to me, "I was sitting alone in the kitchen of the farmhouse, quietly writing letters when there came the sound of contented humming from one corner of the kitchen. I looked up, startled, and listened. Soon I could detect interspersed with the humming, the creaking of a rocking chair. I realized that someone was sitting and rocking in a chair by a far corner window. But it's interesting to note that the kitchen had been redesigned by the former occupants and there was now no room for a chair in that spot. The window was blocked out by modern cabinets.

"The next day I set out to discover if what I suspected had been true. I talked to a neighbor who had known the residents of previous years in that house. Sure enough, I heard that at one time before the cabinets had been put in, the farmwife had kept a rocker by that window and used to sit there frequently.

"Not long after I heard the sounds again. This time I put down my pen and listened carefully. I was able to pick out the tune. It was an old lullaby. I have heard it from that corner many times now. I just sit quietly and enjoy it. It is so 'homey' and charming. It makes me smile to myself with contentment as I sit listening.

"One time I got up and walked as near to the spot as I could get. The tune stopped abruptly and a cold air swept around me like an icy draught from a door opened suddenly. I realized with some remorse what I had done. She didn't care to be interrupted or spied upon.

" 'Whoops!,' I said, 'I'm sorry! Carry on!'

I returned to my chair and the humming started sweetly up again."

Hilda Chance says that so many manifestations occur in this house, it's impossible to speak of them all. But there was one incident not so long ago particularly worthy of telling.

"We found after buying the farmhouse that we needed more spare bedroom space as we have children and grandchildren with us often. So we transformed a storage room on the second floor into a finished and lovely guest room. My husband built a closet in one corner as the room utterly lacked any cabinet space. In that corner a bed had formerly stood but to make room for the closet we turned the bed and backed it against the other wall.

"The night my son arrived we were all sitting in the kitchen having coffee when suddenly we heard the bed above being pushed over the bare floor!

"My son looked at me, wonder in his face. Without thinking, I said, 'She doesn't like the way we placed the bed!' "

" 'Who are you talking about?,' he asked.

"I explained what I meant and told him all about the humming and rocking of the former farmwife.

"Quickly he arose and we followed him up to the room. The bed had been turned. My son moved it back again against the far wall. I found myself looking upwards and carefully explaining, 'Now you see, it must *stay* this way. There's a closet in the corner now and there is no room for the bed there! It must stay here, do you understand?'

"The bed stayed there. It's never moved since."

But, as Mrs. Hilda Chance relates it, other things still move and likely always will for her wherever she lives. She enjoys these "spirit visits" and so why shouldn't supernatural guests continue coming to that lady who is probably the Hostess with the Mostest Ghostes in all the Delaware Valley?

The Haunted Graveyard

If you're out on All Hallows Eve this year, stay a good ways away from an old graveyard in Pennsylvania's Plumstead township.

It stands on a hilltop near old Dublin road and it's haunted.

Leastways that's been the word passed around about it for a good many years.

Take farmer Jonathan Good, for instance, who lived in those parts during the mid 1800's. He was walking past the graveyard on a moonless night that would test the nerves of the hardiest farmer. But he wasn't going to let childish folk tales frighten him. He stuck his hands in his pockets and strode past the graves with the brazen sureness of a crow landing in a cornfield.

Then it happened.

A low moaning crept up along the silence and startled his ears. He stopped walking, so the crunching of his footsteps on the stones ceased.

The moaning grew into a wail and farmer Good felt the flesh tighten on the back of his neck.

It couldn't be . . . yet the sound was there. It came from behind a tombstone off in the darkness to his left. Good strained his eyes and stared at the gawking white gravestones lined up like shimmering ghosts. There was a moment of dead silence.

Then shrieks tore through the blackness.

Jonathan Good swallowed, steadied his knees and his voice and called out. "Who's there?"

The shrieking stopped abruptly as though a ghost were ready to meet a human being at last.

"I am John Hills . . . the man who got killed!"

With that response a figure glided out from behind a grave stone. Good stared at the shadowy figure for a long moment in which his heart seemed to stop beating.

Then he ran. Folk talk or not, this ghost was real. Whoever John Hills was . . . or whoever killed him . . . mattered not to Good. Only getting home and out of the blackness of this witching hour mattered to him now.

The tale spread quickly about Plumstead township and the fear of the old haunted graveyard hovered for years.

Who was the shadowy figure behind the tombstone?

It was no ghost they said. It was the village half-wit, Jack Peidle. The sheriff was sure.

But the stories persisted that a dead man's ghost shrieked through the witching hour at the old Plumstead graveyard.

Unless you dare to find out for yourself . . . stay away!

The Searching Bonaparte

There is nothing left today of the tall, four-storied mansion of Sarah Lukens Keene on Radcliffe Street in Bristol. In its place now stands the modern Margaret Grundy Memorial Library.

But the memory of the great house with its marble mantels, its glimmering paned windows, its frame of surrounding trees still hovers in the thoughts of many of the old residents of the Pennsylvania town.

The tales of its hauntings will never be removed.

But first let us recall the background of the mansion. In the early years of 1800's it was one of the most renown dwellings in the area. Sarah Lukens Keene lived there. Sarah was a beauty. She was young, vibrant, gay — the toast of every gentleman who passed her way. The great portrait painter, Thomas Sully, made her the subject of one of his finest paintings. It hung for years in the oval dining room.

Sarah had many an affair of the heart, it is said. Two men once fought a duel over her on the lawn beside the house. It has never been known who they were or who won or lost the exchange of pistol fire. But neither won the hand of Sarah.

Joseph Bonaparte, ex-king of Italy and Spain, after his brother, Napoleon's fall at Waterloo, escaped to America and built a palace at Bordentown. It is not surprising to learn he was a frequent visitor at the Keene mansion. He would glide down the Delaware on his eight-oared barge and dock at the Keene landing with great pomp and ceremony. Many an evening he dined and wined at the glimmering crystal and silver settings in the oval room. Many an hour he told tales by the snapping fire in the great salon. Often he played at chess or listened to tinkling tunes from the gleaming grand piano in the tall-ceilinged parlor.

It is reputed he looked longingly into the soulful eyes of the lovely Sarah. But she was never to be more than a friend to Joseph Bonaparte.

Whom did Sarah Lukens Keene marry? No one. She gave her heart, it is said, to a man from the hustling city of Philadelphia. A bourgeois man who made beer. Sarah's father put a flat refusal to the courting of his daughter by the beer-maker. Such unworthy a suitor was not to be considered.

The man left Bristol and the gleaming halls of the Keene mansion. And Sarah's eyes never sparkled again. Eventually she was alone in the echoing house. There were no more duelists, no more kings at her hearthside, no more balls and dinners of state. Only the shade trees trembling in cold-fingered winds outside the windows and the still ivory keys of the piano.

Her will said a lot. A lot about loneliness. It left her mansion to the Episcopal Church to be used to care for and house unmarried gentlewomen.

Today only the river-winds brush the grass that was once hers. The lapping of gentle waves tells the story of Bristol's 19th century beauty along the shore where once her satin-slippered feet stepped on and off Bonaparte's barge. The shade trees still hover over Radcliffe Street and recall that once the clicking of swords shattered the night silence on that lawn.

But memories of all these past happenings still haunt the thoughts of many in Bristol. People who recall the Keene mansion. People who knew the old house. People who recall the strange sounds and the eerie moods of the structure which gave it the name it carried for decades: the Haunted House of Bristol.

One of those people is Mattie Byrd. Mattie lives today in Bristol. She was born in Bucks County about 80 years ago. Today her gray hair frames a dark and strong face which smiles graciously at you as she talks. Her posture is straight; her manner dignified, yet warm. Pensively she reflects back on the years she spent in the Keene mansion. Not one of the caretakers would stay there without Mattie.

"It is understandable," she says with a gentle nod of her head. "There was no place more — more shivering and eerie at night than that house."

What did she experience there? What everyone who lived there in recent years did. Footsteps treading distinctly across the floors. Doors opening in the dead of night and clicking shut. Dishes rattling in the kitchen. All sounds and echoes that made one *sure* someone was walking the house at night. But when a night was snapped on — no one would be there. One of the caretakers slept with lights on; few slept at all. It was more than common that two or more would be awake in the night and sit up together. Then the sounds would commence again. One time the snapping of firm steps on the walk outside the house on the river side stalked back and forth all night.

Was this one of the duelists? Did he seek the man who killed him in the darkness of the night so long ago? Was it Boneparte pacing the walk waiting for the lovely mistress of Keene mansion? Does Sarah tread the rooms of her old home, seeking her lost lover?

No one knows the cause of the hauntings, nor who it was who restlessly stirred through the mansion. Perhaps it was all the people who spent happy or sad hours in the magnifiicent home. In the late years of the last century, the Keene mansion was so feared for its hauntings, no one would walk past it. People would cross the street, then back again. Mattie recalls this well.

The newspapers of the day recorded that weird green lights were seen flickering from room to room on darkest nights. It was said to be the ghost of Joseph Boneparte, moving from room to room, lantern in hand, revisiting the scenes and the lovely hostess he admired so much.

Look when you walk along the river's edge behind the Grundy library. Are those green lights shimmering from the water reflections or phosphorous glows? Or are they from the lantern of Boneparte's ghost as he glides on his barge away from a happy evening, drinking to the sparkling eyes of Sarah Lukens Keene?

The Ghost that Died

During the years of the American Revolution a height that arose to the south of Newark, Delaware, was called, "Iron Hill" because of its rich deposits of hematite ore.

At the time of British General William Howe's advance towards the Brandywine in late summer of 1777 it might well have been thought to have earned the name from the great amount of war equipment it bore. Sullen guns, vivid red coats, flashing swords and glistening bayonets appeared among a thick dispersement of tents pitched on all sides.

The British had dug in with a will while working out the strategy for a push into southeastern Pennsylvania and onwards for the capture of Philadelphia.

During the time Howe's forces were entrenched on Iron Hill the Continental Army was trying from its Pennsylvania foothold to outguess the guessers and forestall the strategists. Accordingly, outposts were advanced to the Iron Hill area to reconnoiter and determine as far as possible the strength and disposition of the oncoming British forces.

One of these American outposts was at Welsh Tract Church, a few miles north of Iron Hill. A relay of sentries was set up at the post to assure no surprise attack of their position should occur.

The first sentry assigned to duty just inside the church cemetery wall returned to his quarters after midnight in a state of pale-faced terror. He reported through shivering teeth of having seen a ghost! A white rider on a white horse galloped like streaking lightning straight past him and vanished into the woods beside the church!

The corporal fitting a fat candle into a tin lantern looked up and wiped sweat off his brow. "Methinks you've indulged in more than your rations of ale, lad. Now you be watching your P's and Q's else you be pounding the length of a prison wall instead of a cemetery wall!"

The other men laughed as the sentry took off his hempen shirt and fell onto the floor in the far corner.

"I know what I seen and none of ye can be telling me otherwise!"

The next night the corporal placed another man on duty at the cemetery wall. He was a big shouldered man with arms like blacksmiths' anvils. He grabbed his musket and plunged out into the dark night starting his round with eyes staring sharply all around him. He didn't put much stock in what that other sentry had said. After all, that skinny varmint was a traveling tinker and never had converted very proper to the stuffings needed in a good soldier. He'd spent too many years trudging country roads and his head had been filled with country talk of ghosts and goblins. But himself—well, he'd been a carpenter in Philadelphia and except for loving wild tales of buried pirate gold in tavern cellars or church yard vaults he'd not had much ear for tall stories.

But come the midnight hour and this soldier was shocked into standing lifeless as stone at a sight that froze him to the ground. A white horse came galloping towards him like thunder, bearing on his back a figure robed from head to foot in white. The animal plunged to within ten feet of the wall then veered quickly off to one side and vanished in the woods.

The sentry heaved back into quarters with eyes rolled back in his head.

" 'Tis true! I swear 'tis true! There be a ghost rider plunging through them woods this very minute. I seen him with me own eyes!"

The corporal rubbed his chin whiskers and stared at the man, big as an oak tree, quivering like an aspen in front of him right now.

"I tell you, Corporal, I seen him! I'll fight anything the king sends and anything the meanest devil this side of hell can throw against me, but I can't be fighting something that be not flesh and blood!"

One of the men stretched out on a blanket nearby lifted himself up on one arm. " 'Tis true, Corporal. Whether ye can find the heart to believe it or not, strange creatures haunt these woods. I be living in these parts all my nineteen years and I can tell ye there be Witches' Trees and Goblin Groves. Aye, I myself have heard tell of men seeing horrible forms glowing like burning coals leaping and dancing around great oaks. Once I myself saw shimmering lights swinging ahead of me in the woods as I was coming home from deer hunting one autumn night. A man can't deny what the spirits do on a dark night . . . or laugh at it!"

The first sentry, feeling very much vindicated now sat up and pointed a finger towards the outside. "I say 'tis He who rides the Pale Horse! I say 'tis Death himself coming for us, lessen we pull back to where we belongs! Maybe this pale rider be a sign for just that—"

The corporal glared into the faces of his men. "Maybe it be a sign that your livers be pale!" He snatched his jacket off a wall peg and plunged out into the dark night.

Carefully by the flickering light of his pierced tin lantern he examined the far side of the cemetery wall. There were prints in the dirt of horse's hooves, no mistaking that.

He decided to put the hardest-nosed man in his outfit on guard duty the following night for he himself had to meet with the sergeant to go over reconnoitering plans at first rising of the sun.

A light rain fell that night. "Maybe the bad weather will discourage the Pale Rider," suggested the corporal with a wry smile to his guard. "But keep your eyes open and your powder dry and don't hesitate to shoot no matter what comes charging at you!"

The sentry grinned back, tobacco juice oozing out of the corners of his mouth. He patted the barrel of his musket. "Aye, Corporal. I aims to aim at Mister Death himself, iffen need be!"

The corporal gave a slap to the other man's back. This man had been to sea; been in prison stockades; fought Indians. Tonight, mused the corporal, the story would be different.

It wasn't. The corporal was awakened by the breathless arrival of the sentry back at quarters.

"By the gods, Corporal, something that 'twasn't human came right at me! I could hear the rush of hooves afore I seen anything, so I upped my musket and aimed and fired the minute I seen something but that white horse and rider kept a-coming till near ten feet o' me, then swung away and off they went into the woods. They be not human, I'm certain-sure o' that!"

That night the corporal took the turn of duty himself. He buttoned his collar close under his chin, looked well to the priming of his musket, then withdrew out of the moonlight under the shadows of a large sycamore tree on the far side of the cemetery wall. There he waited. There was no sound but the occasional fall of a drying leaf and the distant hoot of an owl.

Then he heard it. The rhythmic roll of hoofbeats coming across ground, eerie in their precision echoing through the night. In spite of himself a thrill shot up his spine and the hair tightened on his scalp as he stared ahead.

The hoofbeats were louder now. Nearly upon him. The corporal jammed his hat down, set his teeth, raised his flint-look and stepped out of the shadows.

A white figure on a white horse was looming right over him. The sudden appearance of the corporal caused the horse to rear and swerve abruptly; then swing completely around and head back up the path into the half-golden night.

The corporal fired. In the next instant a white form was lying in the dirt and a horse was speeding away towards the hill.

The corporal turned the figure over. A British scout. Under a sheet loosely draped about him, the man wore a cuirass of steel but it had been of no effect in protecting his brain from the corporal's bullet. He was quite dead. At one corner of the worn linen sheet the Continental noticed a hole ripped clean through. The sentry's shot from the night before. A brave one this scout was, thought the corporal as he gazed at the bleeding face.

For a long time afterwards over the Continental campfires and those of the Red Coats, too, the story was told of the daring British scout who had seized on a wild scheme to frighten away the Continental outposts by praying on their rustic fears.

He hadn't counted on a corporal who was convinced this was one ghost who could die.

Thus ends the tale of the only mortal ghost that ever figured in Delaware Valley history.

The Woman in Black

Little six-year-old Ann Reeves pulled the blankets close up under her chin as she shivered. Icy moonlight crackled against the bare branches of the old oak outside, then shattered into her room like a surprise light in a black tunnel.

She steeled herself to peek out above the blankets. Her room was so cold and she was so alone. Yet she was not alone. Long after her mother had tucked her in and the footsteps in the house below had shuffled up the stairs and into the silences of the night, Ann heard sounds. She always did. Not just night noises like the howling of a cat or the snapping of tree branches, but the unheard sounds you feel when someone is near you in the dark.

To this day Mrs. Reeves shakes her head in wonderment. "I never could explain it. I'm not imaginative. I'm a perfectly logical person, but I have no logical answers for what occurred in our old Warminster, Pennsylvania, home."

Young Ann, though, as she lay in her bed one cold night looking about her room lighted up in amber moonlight, was not concerned with logic. She had a feeling; a frightening, overwhelming feeling that someone had again come into her room. Should she leap out of her bed and spring for the door?

Ann peered cautiously out from a corner of her blanket tent. Her chest of drawers stood like a silent giant. Her closet door was wide open and every hanging dress looked about to tremble. Next to the window her searching eyes caught sight of her favorite piece in the room — a blackboard with movable letters of the alphabet at the top. How she loved to swing those letters about and shape new words!

But only when the room was young and bright with friendly morning and she could dance about with chalk in one hand and a cookie in the other and all her dolls could sit smiling at her from the bed.

Now she wanted only to bury herself deeper into the dark coverings about her. But she couldn't. She had to keep searching the room. Someone was in there with her.

A sound pricked at her ears. It came from near the window. Ann moved her head slowly about. Outlined in front of the window, icy with moonlight, was the tall form of an old woman. The black figure waved her arms. Finally, one arm poised in mid-air, her hand moved back and forth across the blackboard, then stopped. The figure turned and faced Ann, then slipped away from in front of the window and vanished. There was nothing now in the room but the big chest, the gaping closet, the sleeping forms of her dolls.

Ann Reeves told her parents the next morning that the old woman had come into her room and had written on the blackboard in the night.

"Nonsense," soothed Mrs. Reeves. "There is no old woman. No one has been in there or been writing anything anywhere."

Mrs. Reeves went to the child's room. It was aglow with yellow sunshine. "How could there have . . ." started Mrs. Reeves. She stopped in the middle of her sentence. Ann had drawn her over to the blackboard by the window. Three letters had been pulled from the alphabet row and still remained to shape a word. "Ann," they said.

After that incident, the child's room was closed off. Ann slept in another room. But that bedroom which was in the old part of the house built in the early 1700's never ceased to bear its haunted character. On several occasions when friends filled the house to capacity, Mrs. Reeves would put a guest for the night in there. Whenever this happened, almost without exception, the guest would ask who came into the room in the night. Several of them explained their restless hours in that room. "I woke up in the middle of the night with a feeling of fright." One of them complained of hearing footsteps up and down the back stairs.

Years later when Ann was in college and came home for vacation, she suggested staying in her old room. She thought with maturity she would not experience the old uneasiness. She was wrong. Each night, as of old, she awoke with an overwhelming sense of fright. "I keep feeling someone has come in," she explained to her mother.

Today Ann is married (she's Ann Hall now), her father passed away and her mother, Mrs. Philip Reeves, sold the old house on York Road and lives in an apartment.

What happened to the house? Reputedly built by Harman Yerkes (his initials were carved in a beam there), the house is now the offices for a stone mason and contractor, Spartacus Olivieri. If you have any doubts about Ann's story, just ask Mr. Olivieri how quiet he found his office? He will then tell you of the curtains billowing out in a room where no draft of air existed. He will tell you of the footsteps his foreman kept hearing on the floor above one night and the search he conducted in which he found every door he had shut upstairs wide open again.

Mr. Olivieri himself spent several terrifying nights there. The doors he had carefully bolted became unlocked. Footsteps creaked so noisily one time he could stand it no longer and plunged out of the house at three in the morning and spent the rest of the night in a local tavern.

Who was the old woman in black? Who walked the creaking floors? Who caused the chill drafts of air that billowed out the curtains? Who locked and unlocked doors?

These are questions that go unanswered along with the child's experience of so many years ago. Why have so many people who have slept in the young Ann's room felt a presence there?

Mrs. Philip Reeves could not find any answers. No one ever has.

Aunt Ellen

There is an old stone house standing off the main road in Trevose, Pennylvania. It stands unobtrusively in the shade of oaks and maples and would not catch the eye of the passerby any more than any other old stone house in the area.

Yet it has a tale to tell that makes a dinner guest look uneasily over his shoulder, put down his fork and gaze motionless at the shining glass panes in the side door of the old house. It is usually about this time, just as the sun is setting and its orange-gold light fills the clear panes of the door—that it happens. The lights in the room grow dim. Then a shadow is seen moving across the door on the outside.

Some member of the family hurries to the door and opens it. There is never anyone there. In another instant the lights in the room blaze back again and all is as it was before with nothing but the faded gold of the disappearing sun filling the door panes.

Sometimes one member of the family has stood waiting at the door for the shadowy apparition to come by. The instant it appeared the door was thrown open. What ghost would be caught? Up and down the pathway, in and out among the trees, the family has searched. Never anyone found.

Who is the shadow at sunset? The story, I was told, relates to a woman who once lived in that house. She is recalled only as Aunt Ellen. She was a determined kind of woman, especially in regard to one thing; she would return to that house after death. She seems to have kept her word. What she hadn't thought of, perhaps, is the uneasiness she has brought to the present-day inhabitants of her home. Children become afraid; their friends are too frightened to call; baby sitters become impossible to obtain. Because of all this, the tale of Aunt Ellen was silenced by the family as much as possible through their years in the house. Few people have ever heard of the story, even in Trevose itself.

Yet will Aunt Ellen let her shadowy story vanish with her into the shades of the old oaks and maples? I doubt it.

Do you doubt it? Do you doubt Aunt Ellen herself, and the passing shadow and the dimming lights?

The family questioned also. The lowering of the lights must be due to a specially heavy load on the main circuit at dinner time, perhaps. The shadow might be the limb of a maple tree shuddering in an evening breeze outside. . . .

Yet it has always *looked* like the form of a woman.

Then one time there happened that unforgettable incident. Just after the shadow had passed and someone jumped up and threw open the door, something was seen. Something golden shone in the last vestiges of sunlight on the side path It was picked up and no-one there has ever forgotten the incident since. It was an old-fashioned bracelet with the initial "E" engraved upon it.

Aunt Ellen was a very determined woman.

Blackbeard's Curse

"Ho, me boys, take down the Jolly Roger and let us send aloft a fancier 'Skull 'n Bones' to strike terror on all who behold us!" Captain Blackbeard tugged on his tar-black beard and spread a yellow-toothed smile across his walnut face.

His men scurried past him on the sloop's deck. In minutes a human anatomy swung in the breeze of the Delaware River. Blackbeard looked up at the skeleton aloft.

"Aye, he makes a goodly banner, boys — as long as he don't spill the rum in his hand!"

The men joined him in raucous laughter that rang along the river banks as their scarlet scarves and golden earrings caught the glow of the setting sun.

Blackbeard unbuttoned his damask waistcoat and placed his huge hands on two pistols hanging at the ends of silk sashes flung over his shoulders. He gazed at the passing shoreline.

He was glad Philadelphia was behind him. Not that the order out for his arrest there that August of 1718 concerned him one noggin's amount. There wasn't a jail large enough to hold him. The Governor of that colony could order all he wanted, there wasn't a man on the City Council or a constable on the streets who would life a nervous finger to carry it out.

The captain spit into the dark waters swirling below and wiped his mouth with one velvet cuff. The point was he had a cargo to tuck safely away and the banks of the Delaware looked like the best spot he'd sighted since he'd gone "on the account" in the North Atlantic waters that summer.

"Sirrah!"

One of his crew was standing at his elbow wrenching the pirate chief out of deep thought. The captain pulled himself up to his full six feet four and swung his 200 pounds of weight about in a fast arc.

"What be ye blabbin' your useless head off for, ye stinkin' scum? Can't ye see I'm thinkin' and layin' plans? — "

The sailor rubbed the patch over one eye nervously. "An't please your lordship, Cap'n, we ain't had a Tryal of our prisoners yet an' they're still below unhang'd!"

Blackbeard spat on the deck and roared. "Harkee, you pitiful dog. Get your Tryal goin' but don't be botherin' me with the scoundrels' prates. I've got me plans to engender 'bout just where we can land our golden cargo. Now fetch me some rum and hang your sun-drying scarecrow prisoners out of me sight whilst I think!"

Blackbeard's boots pounded the deck fore and aft as he watched the shorelines of Pennsylvania; then the curving edge of Jersey. He knew that not far up ahead lay the Manor of William Penn left by its owner some fifteen years before to return to England. On the Jersey side he'd heard scarcely a being could be found but a devout Quaker.

The huge man grunted and scratched his bearded chin. Occasionally the knotted ribbons he tied about the braided strands of his whiskers pulled and itched him. All the same he liked the decoration. Braided beard hairs were his own hallmark. Especially when he thrust in slow-burning matches and set them afire. He roared out loud to himself and his whole frame shook as he thought of the fear he'd seen in his enemies' eyes.

From below he could hear the grating laughter and drunken curses of his crew. He could hear the whining of the prisoners. But what really attracted his attention now was a stretch of shoreline looming up along side of him on the Jersey side. He leaned over the rail with his spy glass.

It was so dark now he could see scarcely more than the thick patterns of full-leaved oaks and towering sycamores. He liked the thick wooded quiet and the selfless-hearted Quakers who owned that land. Of all men, the Friends of Burlington town would be least likely to look for gold.

Captain Blackbeard planted his feet wide apart, braced his two hands on his pistols and waited until the rigging squealed with the scurrying of men aloft. Slowly the ship hove to and its anchor splashed into the inky depths of the Delaware. A full moon arose through the hours that night and lighted the work of Blackbeard and his men as they pulled ashore chests weighty with treasure.

"Here," called Blackbeard as he scratched the moist earth under a large black walnut. "Here we bury the gold and silver for safe-keepin' till we be comin' back to claim it. Heave-to with them shovels me boys; then back to the sloop for a hundred rounds of rum for bed-time peace!"

Just as the last chest was lowered into the pit, black clouds floated over the moon, high winds began to moan in the branches overhead and a sudden storm burst forth in brilliant lightning.

The captain watched as one of his crew lowered a broad flat stone atop the final chest, then he boomed out to his men, the question all pirate crews dreaded to hear.

"Now, me boys, which of ye will guard this wealth?"

The men stirred in their booted feet and licked their lips nervously. There wasn't a man among them who didn't relish a good fight on a sloop's deck but to just step up and be a sacrifice — well that was something else. But buried treasure tradition was inflexible. A man must be interred with the gold to protect it from vandals.

"Sirrah," ventured a Portuguese, "what says ye to takin' one of the prisoners — "

Blackbeard cut him off short. "An' what interest would one of them be havin' in protectin' treasure for us, ye thick-skulled varmint?" Blackbeard stroked his beard with an almost tender touch. "No, me boys, one of ye must have the honor — "

A Spaniard stepped out from a low hanging limb, "Cap'n, I have a suggestion ye may find to your likin' — "

Blackbeard pulled out his right-hand pistol and shot the man clear through the brain.

"I be likin' that suggestion the best of all, me boy!"

The others crowded around, pleased the problem had been solved and set to burying the Spaniard standing up, as was the custom, in ready-to-defend position.

And there, according to Burlington County tradition for over 250 years, the Spaniard still stands under the earth, the treasure beneath his feet, guarding against intruders. On several occasions when treasure-seekers started to dig in that spot a fearful apparition with glaring eyes and a bullet-torn skull arose before them, sending them stumbling back into the woods in terror.

The story also has formed over the years that Blackbeard buried a little black dog with the Spaniard for the ghostly shape of such a creature has been seen from time to time roaming that particular stretch of shoreline at the foot of Wood Street.

The old black walnut under which the gold was buried was last accounted for in the early 1800's as being an "old stump in the Wood Street tanyard." Today nothing is left but the soft lapping of the Delaware waters against the stones and sands of the river's edge. Just as they no doubt licked and splashed against the booted feet of Blackbeard and his crew that summer night so long ago.

The Pooka Comes to Pennsylvania

There were no happier years for Jack Kerigan of Haverford in the last century than those in which he was conductor of the Bryn Mawr band. There were no happier hours than those he spent down with the boys at the old firehall practicing their numbers, honing their skill and their pleasure to a fine edge.

From nearly the very beginning of the time Jack walked from his home to the firehouse for the practice sessions, he noticed a large black dog following in his wake. From time to time, he whistled to it, even leaned over and patted its head on occasion. Then, fearing the winning over of some other person's cherished pet, he tried ignoring it. But to no avail. Every time he'd set out for the practice hall, he'd soon find the black furry animal lumbering along behind him. And he always picked it up—or it picked him up—at the same spot, the corner of Penn Street and Lancaster Avenue in Bryn Mawr.

The dog was soon out of mind, however, the moment the hall came into sight and he'd spot the boys leaning against the wall or exchanging stories and jokes while waiting in the pleasant summer air.

One afternoon, Jack caught sight in a store window of the same black form at his heels. He quickly crossed the street at a snappy pace, for his time was shorter than usual, and hurried on down the block. He flicked a glance over one shoulder and had to smile to himself. The dog was still there, his black eyes glaring up at him like burning coals.

As Jack walked up to the other musicians, with his gaze half on them and half on the furry monster off to his side, he shook his head and smiled softly.

"Sure is one faithful critter!," he said to the others as he kept his eyes on the animal in wonder. "He's been following me for weeks now. Every time I hit that same corner, he's always there. A real Johnny-on-the-spot. What gets me is why? I never feed him or talk to him, yet — "

"Jack! Jack!" called out one of the men. "Who are you talkin' about?"

Jack Kerigan stared unbelieving at his friend.

"I'm talking about this black dog here." He pointed towards the big furry creature beside him.

"What dog? What are you talking about? There's no dog around here."

Jack Kerigan swallowed hard. When he looked down again, the dog was gone. He scratched the back of his head as he followed the boys into the hall and he decided to say nothing more. He never did that night or any other though he continued to see the dog right on schedule at Penn and Lancaster for as long as he was the band's conductor.

"What do you think it is, Mother?," he asked his wife from time to time.

Mrs. Kerigan would only shake her head in wonder. "I can't imagine, dear. I only know strange things do happen in this world."

The Kerigan's daughter, Florence, many years later, was finally the one to supply the answer.

"I read a book by Captain Diarmuid MacManus called, *The Earth People of Ireland*. He talked about the spirits and elementals of Ireland and Wales who guard fairy places from mortal trespassing," Florence Kerigan tells you today. "I wrote him about my father's experience and he explained that the 'Pooka', a large black dog or pony that pursues one or more members of a family is a fierce defender against trespassers and was no doubt the creature following father."

This shaggy animal that Mr. Kerigan saw, the daughter went on to explain, probably came over from the old country with the migrating family.

All of which is a most acceptable explanation to this Irish lass whose blue eyes twinkle like fairy lights as she talks of this startling and unusual creature so part of her family's past.

There came a time when Florence Kerigan discovered the pursuing Pooka was, indeed more than legend. She was on her way to the local library when she felt something close behind her. She turned. Right on her heels was a large shaggy-coated black dog. His eyes were glowing like hot coals as he stared up at her. He never left her. She reached the library.

A man was holding open the door, waiting for her.

"I hope the dog won't try to follow me in," she commented softly.

"What dog?," asked the man.

Florence Kerigan smiled to herself. The Kerigan Pooka was back!

Breakfast for Two

One morning, a few decades ago, a group of children on horseback crunched through the woods of Wrightstown, Pennsylvania. A stream wound beside their bridle path sending a morning mist swirling around the horses' hooves.

The group rounded a bend. Their gay voices dropped to a hush. Before them rising from the mist like an Ivanhoe castle, was a fieldstone house built like a fort. Its high walls with windows protected by grating loomed over them like a gray ghost. Most of the roof was gone. Only dead vines still clung to the rusted window bars.

"That's the Haunted House!" shrilled one of the riders.

"Sure," agreed another. "That's the old Collitt Mansion. Been deserted for years. Ever since old man Collitt and his wife died."

One of the girls gasped, "Look!" All eyes wide open followed her outstretched arm. One the weed-spotted terrace beside the house where it was said the Collitts loved to have breakfast, rested now a table. It was fully set with silver, plates and goblets for two.

"Gosh!" exclaimed all the children at once.

With a dig of their heels into the horses' shanks, the early morning riders wheeled and clattered back to the stable.

From that day on, enrollment in the riding academy doubled. The number of picnickers and hikers in the township increased immeasurably. The favorite outdoor sport of nearly everybody in the area became a trip to the Haunted House. None, though, it is said, dared to explore after dark.

There are few residents left in the area who remember Mr. Collitt. He was a grizzly man who wore baggy clothes and a scrunched-up hat even when he went to work in Philadelphia. He was a patent lawyer for a city firm, but a wild-eyed inventor on his own, once he reached his home in Wrightstown for the week-end.

It was a real experience, a local garage owner once related, when he drove Mr. Collitt home from the Friday evening train. It was a harrowing trip just to get there, so deep in the woods had he built his "castle." Usually the barn door would open revealing a Stanley Steamer, half apart; or a stack of typewriters in varying degrees of dismantlement.

The castle was intriguing to any visitor. It was well-guarded by a deep hole dug right beside the front door, which, if its presence was not known, could trap an unwary guest on a dark evening. Mr. Collitt didn't have the reputation of not caring for callers for nothing.

Inside the house was an equally challenging experience. The roof gaped wide open in places which served to give plenty of air-conditioning in the summer to the Collitts. Instead of hard wood laid down for flooring most of the rooms had only rough planks stretched across the frame work. The windows were all covered with iron grating, slightly reminiscent of the dungeon of the Castle Chillon.

After the death of Mr. Collitt in the early years of this century, Mrs. Collitt lived alone for some years. After her passing the castle slipped slowly into disrepair. Some years ago it burned down. Fire consumed all the furnishings, fireplace mantels, cobwebs and ghost tales.

No more does anyone hear of the ghostly sight of the breakfast table set for two on a deserted terrace.

Who set the "ghost table?" Was it a smart riding school promotion? Was some neighbor a practical joker? Or did the unique Mr. Collitt and his wife refuse to give up their provocative ways even after death?

No one has ever supplied the answer. Only the shaking trees in the woods of Wrightstown witnessed the deed and they have never told.

The Groom from the Tomb

In the years which followed the close of the Revolution, Philadelphia exploded into a post-war boom that shook the city's conservative foundations. Dignitaries from here and abroad came to visit and often stayed for good, so pleasing was the fast-growing luxury in the new nation's capital.

Homes of faithful patriots were no longer settings for plottings and intrigues and tea-less tea parties. They were meccas of lavish entertainments and delicacies of living. Estates such as that of William Bingham's three-acre spread in center Philadelphia were aglow with marble stairways, expensive Italian paintings, French wallpaper, English carpets and expensive gold furniture accented by outside gardens aromatic with tropical orange trees.

The favorite activities of Philadelphians included drinking, gambling, dining and dancing. Quaker simplicity had become lost in the new-found freedom of a once chained country. With old restrictions relaxed, no new ones took form.

"An attractive scene of debauchery and amusement," was the comment made by Richard Henry Lee of the new era city. Although the President and Lady Washington held levees and teas of dignity and good taste, other socialites were setting a new trend for entertainment. It was not only highly acceptable in the revived City of Brotherly Love to drink to excess, it was the demand of the day. Most hosts would lock the door and refuse to allow a guest to depart until heavily intoxicated. At one festivity, it was recorded that 80 guests consumed 45 huge punch bowls and 22 bottles of liquors and crab cider. General Nat Greene wrote of attending a dinner in which he was served 160 different dishes.

Gambling ranked high among the entertaining pursuits of the times also. Losing several hundred dollars at a sitting was a common thing for the social set. Dances, balls and masquerades that consumed countless dollars and hours in preparation were only so many more delights to the "cream-set" of the capital.

"It is too much," frowned the good Quakers and God-fearing citizens. "God will afflict the city with His wrath!"

Superstition? Perhaps so. No one can say. What did occur, though, is history and it came swift and terrible in the summer of 1793. The Quakers of the day labeled it, "retribution."

The trouble had begun in the spring. It had been a wet and blustery April and May. Colds, mumps and scarlet fever had caused more than the usual upset. With summer came very little sun; still more rain. The gutters flanking the city's streets were never dry but full to the rims with stagnating water. On the outskirts of the city swamps were overflowing with putrid water. By August the residents of Philadelphia were forgetting their parties and picnics and taking to their beds with fever, headaches and sore throats. Their eyes were bloodshot; their pulses fast.

Doctors were at a loss to diagnose. So they did the next best thing: they kept their patients drunk with brandy, covered with blankets soaked in vinegar; their limbs coated with plasters. They prescribed blood-lettings and goodly doses of Peruvian bank. Still no progress.

Suddenly as skins turned yellow, it became clear. The dreaded plague had hit Philadelphia — Yellow Fever.

No one knew how to check it. Dedicated doctors devoted themselves to tireless rounds of their patients' houses. Men like Stephen Girard helped evacuate the ill to temporary hospitals. Scientists of the day wiped their brows and pored over books, throwing out one desperate suggestion after another.

As a result bonfires were set all over the city as a recommended action for purifying the air. Gunpowder, it was announced, would act as a preventative so guns and muskets were heard crackling from backyard to backyard all through the day. Revolutionary cannon were hauled out from their arsenals and dragged up and down the streets. Frightened citizens inside their homes were puffing on cigars or trying new measures of safety: stuffing their pockets with garlic and even taping it to the skin in hopes it would ward off infection. Others wore camphor bags and drank tar water.

Still others, who had the means, pulled stakes and left the city in sensible haste. President and Lady Washington were fortunately already in Germantown where they were accustomed to spending the summer months in the Morris House on Market Square. Tom Jefferson went on the prowl along with thousands of others and felt himself most fortunate to locate a cot in a corner of a tavern for $8 a night.

Germantown became filled to the brim with refugees. Its streets, too, became the scene of 24-hour bonfires and the air was alive with the snapping of gun fire to prevent the spread of infection.

Well-known for some time as a fashionable community since its heroic war years, Germantown was now serving as the temporary capital of the nation. Among the important figures who lived in the town was the Billmeyer family.

Michael Billmeyer was the official printer for the Pennsylvania Assembly and a man of means and stature. He built and owned several homes in Germantown. Among them was a new addition which in that summer of 1793 he had just had constructed on a house on Germantown Pike that had been built for his son, Daniel.

That summer a legend arose for that Daniel Billmeyer house which it bears to this day. An engaged couple rented it from Mr. Billmeyer. It was the perfect setting, the young girl felt, for a bride and groom. It was serene in the midst of the fear-freezing horrors of that summer with its cool fanlights, its hand-carved doorways, its fragrant garden awash with sweetness from its roses and patterned with wisteria vine and cool-to-the-touch English ivy shimmering on its south wall.

Mr. Billmeyer felt there could be no better first-occupants of his new addition than the newly-wedded. He handed over to the bright-eyed girl the great shining key to the brass lock on the front door.

Within a short time she had moved in. Band boxes and ribbons and a gleaming new leather chest were all carried in as she took over as mistress.

Then her promised one arrived in his carriage and carried in his leathern cases and chests filled to a goodly weight with his books and clothes and endless treasures.

" 'Tis only till the morrow, dear love," his bride-to-be said as she walked with him through the rooms, "and we will be mistress and master here together. See how light the house is, even though the day be dark." She pointed up to a high fan window with childish delight.

Together with shoes off, they roamed through the big kitchen below with the huge open fireplaces large enough to hold two cranes and a hundred cooking pots. They ran in circles; then fell laughing to the dirt floor where they dug their toes into the cool grains.

At the front door later the young girl lifted her face to her promised. "I love thee, forever."

"And I love thee till the day I die and beyond e'en that, I promise thee." The young man leaned down and kissed her. "I can't wait till the morrow; till I can claim my bride for the rest of my life!"

After the big door closed shut, the young girl skipped up the stairs to the bedchamber. Tenderly and with humming from her lips, she unpacked her bridal gown and set it across a chair back till the morrow.

The dress remained where it was, untouched for countless months. The young girl never put it on. Never spoke her vows in it, for her lover never came back. He was struck down with fever that night before their wedding and died.

The young bride-to-be never got over the tragedy. And, according to legend, neither did the groom. 'Tis said, any bride who spends the night in the master chamber upstairs, to this day, can hear the footsteps of that long dead groom climbing the stairs to claim his new wife.

Today Mrs. Manning Smith lives in the old Billmeyer house. She reports that once, when her daughter was a bride and spent the night there, the young girl heard footsteps come quickly up the stairs; then slowly descend down the back steps.

For a moment, perhaps, 1793 had come once again.

The Weeping Woman of Smithtown

Smithtown, on the Delaware Canal in Pennsylvania, catches the eye of every passerby. Its worn bridge presents a picturesque scene. The utterly motionless form of the lazy canal stretches green and serene alongside the river road. On the opposite bank of the canal, old stone houses rest apart from the busy life of the passing traveler. They stand between the canal and the Delaware river at peace with the world.

But not all of the hours in the life of Smithtown are as calm as the passing moment would make one believe. The riverbank there shelters among its concealing trees and brush the most forlorn of ghosts. It is the form of a woman. Sometimes she is seen pacing the river's edge among the lacy patterns of moonlit tree branches. Sometimes she is only heard. The sound of her weeping at dusk fills the quiet river air after the birds have settled to quietness.

Who is this who paces and cries in mournful tones as she wrings her hands, gazing intermittenly across the river? It is the ghost of Mrs. Edward Marshall, as any old-time resident of the area knows. Her story goes back over two centuries.

Edward Marshall lived on the river bank in this area in the early 1700's. He worked with surveyors. He was a chain-carrier marking out distances for surveyors with a chainlike instrument which measured 66 feet long. In this capacity he developed love and understanding of the wilderness. He knew every inch of his environs. He was also used to the rigors of exposure and had developed stamina far beyond even the great strength of his contemporaries who were all woodsmen and hunters.

In the late summer and early fall of the year 1737 a momentous event in history was taking shape. The northern borders of William Penn's land grant from the Lenni-Lenape Indians was being decided upon. William Penn had long since been gone, but his two sons, Thomas and John Penn, had, unlike their noble father, come to be dissatisfied with the agreements made between the Penns and the Indians. They wanted more land. To accomplish this end they devised a scheme that has since been the blackest mark on the Delaware Valley's history.

The Penn boys produced, so they said, a document which had been agreed upon by their father and the Lenni-Lenapes in William Penn's lifetime here. It stated that the extent of the land of Penn's purchase went from Wrightstown "as far as man can go in a day and a half". To determine now exactly where the northern boundary lay, were the Indians agreeable to fixing the place by just the methods Penn had prescribed — the distance a man could walk in a day and a half?

The Indians were used to such terms. They had done it frequently with Penn. They would walk leisurely along together, stopping for rests along the way.

Thomas and John Penn had other ideas in mind. One of the first of these was to obtain the services of Edward Marshall, the chain-carrier, as a "walker" for the occasion. They also hired James Yeate, an agile athlete, and another local man known for his superior strength, Solomon Jennings. The Indians were then notified of when and where to meet. It was at Wrightstown at sunrise on the morning of September 19, 1737 (the spot is now marked by a monument). Thus began the event since known as the Infamous Walking Purchase.

The Indian walkers started, as was customary, strolling peaceably along the ground, expecting to pass a word or two with the white men as they ambled. Other Indians walked along as observers. Volunteers also accompanied the expedition, bearing food for the participants.

It soon became clear that the white men were not planning either to talk, rest or eat. They stepped up their pace faster and faster. Immediately the Indians protested. They were ignored. The white men pushed on at a run. Gradually the expedition followers fell back. Some of the Indian walkers fell far behind. The three white men seared wildly through the brush. At what is now Ottsville, one of the last of the Indians dropped and Jennings gave out. Yeates and Marshall continued.

At the place now known as "Gallows Hill", Marshall is said to have broken his suspenders jumping a creek and that he hung his "gallowses" on a bush, giving that region its present name. Soon the third and last Indian quit. After camping overnight not far from the Lehigh Gap, the two hired walkers pushed on the next morning. While crossing a stream Yeates fainted. Marshall continued on alone. By noon of the second day, Marshall had reached a place about three miles from present day Mauch Chunk or Jim Thorpe, as it has been more recently called. Here Marshall seized hold of a young sapling and dropped exhausted. The Walking Purchase was over.

But not its effects. For generations after, the cheating of the Lenni-Lenapes in that walk stirred enmity. The Indians had been robbed of thousands of acres of land. The walk effected the lives of the Indians, the whites, the walkers, and, of course, the walkers' families. No one could have testified more poignantly to that than Edward Marshall's wife.

After the affair was over and its dishonest intent clear to the Indians, no one who had had anything to do with the walk was safe in the environs. The Indians were searching for blood in revenge.

Edward Marshall knew this as well as anyone. He fled.

Perhaps history can not blame the chain-carrier for the walk itself. He was doing a job. But the black mark against Marshall springs from the flight from his home. He flew to safety, leaving his wife and children unprotected in their stone home on the riverbank.

Mrs. Marshall was not afraid at first. She wanted Edward safe. But when she began to hear of the cries for vengeance uttered by the enraged Indians, she began to look for Edward's return. He would come back to protect them from the attack which was, without doubt, imminent.

Hour after hour, day after day, Mrs. Marshall left the children in the house and walked to the river's edge, searching for her husband. He never came.

One day the chilling cries of Indians descending on the area told her the hour had come. She bolted windows and doors. But the Indians made splinters of every shutter. Finally she pressed the children down into the cellar. She closed the door behind her, bolted it and huddled with the children in her arms in the far corner. Even as she heard the footsteps overhead and the door shatter to bits, she must have held one last hope that her husband would return. There could have been no time for one further thought. Mrs. Marshall and her children were massacred and left heaped in the corner of the damp, dirt-filled cellar.

Edward Marshall did return. Much too late, of course. His graves lies in a cemetery high on a hillside overlooking the river and his old house which still stands in Smithtown Colony.

Mrs. Marshall returned, too — as a ghost. For over two centuries she has returned to that spot on the riverbank from which she watched so long those last days of her mortal life. Her vigil is still in vain. No one comes. She walks to and fro, wringing her hands. And the sound of her weeping is heard at dusk when the birds have settled to silence and the river mists are heavy.

Today the Marshall dwelling still stands as one of the oldest and best preserved houses along the Delaware. It is owned by a retired Navy officer, Commander Manila Barber, who reports with snapping brown eyes and a bemused smile that she has, indeed, heard footsteps pacing back and forth in the dead of night.

It was when she first moved into the house. Through an open window on the second floor she heard the precise pattern of slow-walking feet. With a fast-beating heart and a stout-beamed flashlight she searched the grounds and swept the roof lines with her light. She could find nothing.

"I've always felt it was some kind of large animal but all the same, the sound of that slow pacing was strongly suggestive of human footfalls. I've never forgotten it."

Perhaps, as with Mrs. Edward Marshall, frightening experiences in that house are not easily lost from thought.

Midnight Mary

When it is spring, it is prom time for most teenagers. It is the unforgetable hour of life when hearts that meet come closer together or, perhaps, forever drift apart.

But for the young people of Bristol, Pennsylvania, it is more than all these things. It is remembrance, too. A memory that always comes back again. The memory of a senior prom a few years back. It is a recollection that is literally a haunting thing.

It is the memory of that high school prom in Bristol when a pretty girl named Mary danced the evening through in the arms of her best boyfriend, her soft dress swinging this way and that, like a delicate Japanese lantern swaying in the wind.

Late that evening with a midnight sky dark overheard, the young couple started for home. The car sped easily over streets washed by a rain that had come and gone. Along the edge of Tullytown lake outside of Bristol they glided swiftly.

Then it happened. No one is sure just why or just how. The car spun off the road and into the water, sinking slowly into the dark silence. The boy escaped. But not a trace of the girl was ever found. The sad end to Mary and her dream prom have become a nightmare to Bristol. For Mary will not stay gone and forgotten.

How can this be?

Ask the young couple who saw her once as they were circling the lake. Suddenly as they were staring at the water a form arose out of the darkness and glided toward them. It was Mary in her floating prom dress. The young girl watching fainted and the boy hurried home with a tale so strange he scarcely knew how to tell it.

Ask the trucker who was driving along the highway a few years ago and saw a young girl standing by the side of the road looking toward him wistfuly for a lift. He stamped on the brakes. It was unbelievable. What would a wisp of a girl in a frothy bit of gown, dripping wet, be doing alone on a highway at midnight? He pushed open the far door. The girl climbed up and sat down next to him. She said not a word, but arranged her dress gently beneath her, and stared straight ahead.

The driver closed the door for her and started up. He asked her where she was headed. There was no answer. He was blinded for a moment by the strong headlights of an on-coming car. Then all settled down into quiet blackness and a clear highway ahead. "Any special place you wanta be dropped off at, Miss?"

He turned his head for a quick glance at the frail figure that had settled so gently at his side a moment before.

The seat was empty. In her place was a pool of water.

Ask some of the high school students of Bristol township who went up one midnight after a dance to Tullytown lake and waited tense and listening on a moonlit night. Suddenly, something, pale and shimmering, danced across the water.

It was the light from the Fairless Steel plant, insist the parents who heard of the incident. But the young people of the area whisper only of the return of Mary dancing by the light of the moon, swaying this way and that in her wisp of a gown, like the gentle swinging of a Japanese lantern in a spring wind.

Midnight Mary, as she is called, comes back from time to time, to dance once again at a Bristol prom. Her feet will not rest.

Neither can her friends who know that any moonlit night the hour of twelve may be prom time again . . . for pretty Mary . . . at the edge of Tully-town lake.

The Ghost of St. James Street

In the last century there was a narrow, three-storied house on St. James Street near 13th in Philadelphia that challenged all its neighbors when it came to attention-getting. Other houses in the neighborhood may have been larger and more imposing but how many could boast of spine-chilling cries floating through its walls or terrible dragging sounds down the stairs or a door that creaked and groaned when no one was near it?

This little house could brag of all that and did. It soon earned the singular reputation of being called the "Haunted House of St. James Street."

It was, as most ghostly homes are, the setting for a horrifying reenactment of a long-ago tragedy. The tale was told and retold in Philadelphia for over a century. It was repeated in husky whispers beside low-burning coal fires; beneath gaunt midnight-chiming clocks or under dark eaves in some upper bedroom by children too frightened with the telling to get to sleep.

Was that a groan from the bedroom door? the children would wonder in their various homes. Was that a sound from the hallway below? No, no, they would reassure themselves, such weird happenings belonged only to that coffin-narrow house on St. James Street!

So it seemed from time to time and from house to house that the frightening St. James ghost might be making his way from portal to portal along the streets of that area.

But the Ghost of St. James Street never really wandered beyond the slim confines of the old place where he was born. Like most reliable ghosts, this soul-weary; heart-torn fellow lingered at the spot of his demise, the sad event that took place on a dark night in the 1840's. He had fought with another man for the love of a woman. It was a tragic contest. It was his last engagement with an adversary. He was killed.

Yet, perhaps, not quite. Not forever did the young man, it would seem, give up his right to fight for what he wanted. If reports of occupants of that house in subsequent years are to be believed, the young combatant did not give up at all. He came back over and over and fought again and again that very same match over an affair of the heart.

So it was for years afterwards, late at night when silence had fallen over the house, various occupants of the upper chambers would hear the door to the back room begin to strain and creak as though being pulled and pushed and plucked by a dozen spirit forces from all directions. Through every nail, down the stretch of heavy paneling and from each hinge issued groaning and thumping as though some weight were being thrown against it periodically. Then a scraping sound cut into the darkness similar to fingernails clawing at the door planks. Then, finally, it would give way slowly, ever so slowly, as though the catch had gently become disengaged and with effort the door being pushed open from the inside.

Once wide open, new eerie noises poured over the threshold. Soft, dragging sounds and heavy breathing telling of some near-helpless individual pulling himself painfully across the hall floor towards the stairs. From here the sounds descended the stairway—one, two, three—and on downwards. With each dragging thump, the listeners felt their hearts leap into their throats with transformed agony. Someone was wounded. Was dying. Was trying to save himself and get to help on the outside—

When the chamber doors would fly open and the occupants would peer cautiously at the dim stairway flickering faintly under the glow of their oil lamps, they would see nothing. The narrow staircase was quiet and shadow-padded as if nothing out of the ordinary had occurred. Pursuing down the steps and looking out the front door into the empty street of St. James never offered any further clues.

People who experienced the blood-chilling drama thought, at first, horrible nightmares were responsible. If so, then the nightmares, so common to various residents of the St. James house, were an oddity unto themselves.

On other occasions, residents claimed they heard, as the sounds dragged down the steps and reached the bottom, the additional hair-raising noise of terrible cries calling out to the darkness in vows of vengeance.

Whatever occurred—both in life or, perhaps, as rumored, in after-life, in the narrow-framed house on St. James Street is buried deep now in a forgotten past. The haunter, the haunted and the house itself are all gone today.

The Man at the Stairway

In 1945 when Grace and Arthur Pope moved into the brick house on North Stockton Street in Trenton, New Jersey, they did so hurriedly and for a tragic reason. A fire had wiped out their old home and upholstery shop taking along as well the life of their three year old son, Jimmy.

Setting up business once more and picking up the threads of existence were not easy to do but necessary, for life had to be lived; business had to go on as there were customers to be satisfied and more than all that, they still had the treasure of a one-and-a-half year old daughter, Penny, to live for and to cherish.

Grace found that more and more, due to Arthur's failing health, she had to be working in the upholstery shop downstairs. But as she sewed long hours in the workroom she would keep her ears alert for sounds of Penny playing in her bedroom upstairs.

One day as Grace was fitting some fabric to a large sofa back she became aware that the sound of Penny's feet was scurrying faster than usual and in a different place. The patter of tiny feet didn't stay in one spot but was scooting at a quick pace along the hallway upstairs.

Grace held still for a long moment, listening, pins gripped firmly between her lips. Was the child near the top of the stairs, at the small landing area that connected the master bedroom with the kitchen? She started to rise from her work stool when something at the foot of the stairs to the left and slightly behind her caught her eye.

A man was standing there. He was elderly with a thin, parchment-pale face and he was looking up the stairs that were out of sight behind the workroom wall to Grace. In the next instant, he turned and looked over at her with soulful, deep-set eyes.

Grace Pope hurried over to where he was standing with a sense of wonder sweeping over her. Who was he? Had a customer come into the building without her being aware of it?

Just as she approached him, he faded into shadowy air and she found herself alone at the foot of the stairway.

Penny was, as she could now see upon looking up, running back and forth across the landing above, scurrying happily from the bedroom to the kitchen and back again.

Hmm, thought Grace, the child had learned a new game. She ran up and took the child by the hand into the kitchen and busied her with a stack of pots and pans to bang about on the floor. Then she closed the kitchen door firmly and returned to her workroom below.

She combed the dusky corners of the downstairs for sight of the old man but there was no one there. She didn't really expect there to be for Grace Pope was a woman of acute sensitivity in the world of the Sixth Sense, and she felt deeply that the person she had just seen was no ordinary man. But who he was or why he had appeared to her, she did not know.

Mrs. Pope went back to her fitting work and decided to say nothing about the strange incident to anyone for a while.

The next day as she was sewing a seam into some tapestry fabric and the machine was humming away, she suddenly felt a presence behind her again. She looked up quickly and there he was. Almost simultaneously, she realized Penny's footsteps were crossing and recrossing above again.

The minute Mrs. Pope approached the old man's figure, dressed in what looked like a dark dressing gown, he vanished.

The next morning as Grace was cooking breakfast, the same feeling came over her of someone's being nearby. She looked into the hall just in time to catch sight of the elderly gentleman, looking straight at her with a beseeching gaze in his eyes. Then he glanced down the steps and quickly vanished as little Penny came wheeling around the corner and toddled eagerly towards her mother in the kitchen.

Grace poured out some milk for her daughter and as she handed it to the chubby pink fingers she had to smile with a sudden sweet thought. Of course, that man appeared every time her little girl was near the top of the steps! He was afraid for the child's life — afraid that she might fall down the stairs! He was there to warn her!

That evening when Arthur returned with two workmen in the pickup truck from delivering a set of armchairs, Grace spoke to him about putting up a fence gate at the top of the stairs. Agreeing that the idea was a good one and a necessary one now that the child was learning the sport of running around the upstairs, Arthur had the flexible wooden gate attached to the stair wall by early the next morning.

Now Grace could relax as she sewed and the tiny footfalls clipped back and forth above. All was secure and she smiled to herself at the whole unusual chain of circumstances. Although she watched the foot of the steps off and on all the day, the old man never came back.

Until the following day when one of the workmen who had helped carry the sofa into the pickup came back for a moment to use the bathroom upstairs. While he was up there, suddenly the old man appeared at the foot of the stairway again. His dark form caught the corner of Grace's eye and she was looking once again into a pair of anxious eyes.

The gate at the top of the stairs must be open!

Grace ran up. Sure enough, the workman had left it in open position. She quickly closed it and immediately the man below disappeared.

From that time on, whenever helpers or visiting friends would go upstairs, Grace always knew whether or not they had obeyed her instructions to close the gate after them. For although the stairway was out of sight to her and everyone knew it, she always was aware when the gate was open for Bing! just like that! the old man would appear.

It got to be a joke with the workmen. In a hurry, half the time the men would not bother to close the gate until they were going down, but they found they could not fool Mrs. Pope. The minute they'd leave the fence back against the wall, they'd hear Mrs. Pope call up, "Shut the gate!"

The constant wonder in those men's minds was always: How could she know?

One day, curious as to the identity of the old man, Grace Pope began to ask around the neighborhood about the family who had lived there before them. One neighbor had known them well. The father of one of the spouses lived there with the family. He was a kindly old gentleman of whom everyone was very fond. Then a tragedy occurred. One night when the old father got up in the night to go to the bathroom he must have lost his bearings in the dark. He fell down the flight of steps and was killed.

Grace Pope returned to her sewing machine after this knowledge with deep feelings. She felt a kinship with this man in his sadness and a love for him, too. A love for a person she'd never met or known in life.

"But we came to know each other in this tender mutual concern we shared for little Penny. I, in my active life here on earth; he, in his After-Life from where he so easily stepped to visit me and look after my Penny."

Always the recollection of this man has been a fond one. Grace Pope, only a few short years after this incident, was widowed. She is Grace Walker today and a "sensitive" or medium warmly and widely known in the Delaware Valley area.

The U.S.S. The Sullivans . . . Specter Ship

Ghost ships have sailed through countless centuries of sea lore. But how many have rocked innocently at dock in the Philadelphia Navy Yard?

Only one, it would seem, if sailors' sights and sounds are to be believed . . . a unique destroyer that's putting the "Mothball Fleet" into the crystal-ball class.

She is the U.S.S. THE SULLIVANS, of World War II vintage, in a rank by herself for several reasons. She carries the only plural form of a name in the present U.S. Naval fleet; she bears an insignia on the main deck and the forward stack . . . a bright, green shamrock . . . and her name is imprinted on the fantail in Kelly green.

But that's not all. She floats a phantom tale through every barracks and into even the most resistant officers' ward room at the Base. Try as Navy officials will to squelch the stories with worldly reasoning, THE SULLIVANS' specters are reputed to wander down the deserted passage ways and darkened decks of the "dead" ship.

The ghostly tales are born of a heroic past. For one who might not recall one of the bloodiest South Pacific battles of World War II, a bronze plaque aboard the destroyer, mounted on the foreward bulkhead of the after deckhouse, reminds the present of the past. The ship is named in honor of five brothers who went down on the light cruiser U.S.S. JUNEAU in the Battle of Guadalcanal: Joseph, Francis, Albert, Madison and George Sullivan.

The fateful day began portentiously. It was Friday the 13th . . . in November of 1942. Rear Admiral Daniel J. Callahan, in command of a fleet of U.S. ships in the South Pacific, had an assignment. He was to block the arrival of the fast-moving "Tokyo Express," a task force of Japanese ships under the command of Admiral Hiroaki Abe, "down the slot," headed for Guadalcanal. Abe's mission? To wipe out the American base, Henderson Field, and slaughter the Marines there with high explosive shells.

What Admiral Abe didn't figure on was the presence of a U.S. Navy van in Ironbottom Sound. Its ships were lighter and fewer, but they had an advantage . . . surprise.

Then, no one knows why, Admiral Callaghan committed an error. Paralleling the Japanese van, he neglected to change course and swing over to cross the enemy's "T" when his radar contact first showed the approach of Abe's forces.

Instead, unexpectedly, the leading destroyer of the U.S. screen suddenly sighted two Japanese destroyers about to cross her bows. She swung hard-a-port to avoid a collision. This maneuver threw the American column into disorder. Callaghan delayed eight minutes before ordering gunfire for fear of hitting his own ships. Confusion was rampant. The element of surprise was lost. And in that precious eight minutes the Japanese had time to remove their bombardment shells from their decks (which, if hit, would have completely destroyed them) and replace the ammunition with armor-piercing shells necessary for sea battle.

In a few minutes the Japanese searchlights picked out the American line and several of our ships were sent down. Admiral Callaghan, Admiral Scott, their staffs, and countless men were killed.

The battle that ensued stands out in naval history along with the desperate sea fights of the 17th century when each side slugged away at the other until all but one ship went down.

It was not only a night of unlucky portent; it was moonless and black. Neither side was sure whom he was hitting. It was a wild melee in darkness lit up occasionally by flashes of gunfire, torpedo explosions and star shells.

Four bells of the midwatch struck at the height of the battle. Survivors fought on. Green flare lights, white bursts from exploding magazines, and the red and white trails of tracer shells were their only gliding lights in a hell of black smoke and oil fires.

At 0226 the captain of the HELENA, the senior undamaged cruiser, ordered all ships able to do so to retire via Sealark Channel. Only the SAN FRANCISCO, JUNEAU and three destroyers could obey the command. It was a pathetically small surviving force.

Although the remaining limping ships pulling outwards didn't know it, it was to become still smaller.

The men were not in bad spirits aboard the JUNEAU as she pushed through the channel, listing heavily. The five Sullivan boys, like all the sailors, were counting their blessings. The battle was over. They were alive. They were on their way to Espiritu Santo in New Hebrides for rest. Thence they'd forge on to Pearl Harbor for repairs. These thoughts brought laughter and back slapping from the most fatigued. The proverbial pleasures of wine, women and song awaited them.

These were the near-last thoughts of 700 men on board the light cruiser. It was struck suddenly by a torpedo from a submarine strong amidships. The JUNEAU went down in minutes. Only ten men lived to tell the tale. The five Sullivan boys were not among them.

And yet — Joseph, Francis, Albert, Madison and George do tell the tale. So it is said . . . on moonless nights and especially on a Friday the 13th when the ship named for them creaks and sighs at her restraining dock ropes in the Philadelphia Navy Yard.

Like the other ships in the U.S. Navy "Mothball Fleet," THE SULLIVANS rests listless at dock with no machinery whirring, no wood groaning, all doors sealed with fibre glass . . . within, a strictly controlled, dry air environment is disturbed only by periodic routine inspections to make sure the ship is ever in a state of readiness to be activated if needed, as in the case of the battleship NEW JERSEY.

It is from out of one of these routine check-ups the weird tales began to unfold. What better substance to shape a phantom than the soundless dark of a "dead" destroyer? The most spine-chilling ghost could ask no more.

It all started a few years ago when an electrician's mate was ordered to go on board THE SULLIVANS and look over the flooding system. He did that which is never done. He refused.

The commanding officer found he had more than a disciplinary problem. He had a ghost to deal with. It seems, according to the sailor, a specter or specters haunted the passageways, convincingly enough to grab an intruder by the ankles and scare the starch out of him! He should know. It happend to him. The officer was astonished at the genuine terror of the sweat-washed skin and white-rimmed eyeballs before him.

It was a joke, he explained. Fellow sailors having fun with him in an invitingly mysterious situation.

The electrician's mate shook his head. No sir! It was Friday the 13th and he wasn't taking any chances. Those five boys would be coming back for sure on bad-luck Friday and they didn't always wait for that, either. Black moonless nights did just as well for their ghostly wanderings. . . .

Many another sailor has nodded his head in agreement. Pranksters are not a convincing solution to the many weird incidents that have occurred on board that destroyer with the bright green shamrock, they say. Lights flicker on and off, just as the star shells flashed through the darkness in Ironbottom Sound nearly 30 years ago, when the Sullivan boys were fighting till the blood and the sweat poured down their faces.

Other things happened, too. One electrician discovered that his tool box had disappeared right from under his nose. Another sailor claims to have seen five luminous forms floating ahead of him down a passageway pitched in darkness. Other men come off the ship unnerved from inexplicable noises and groans following them in the sealed-off interior. Although Navy safety regulations require men to work on the ships in pairs, one hashmarked veteran had occasion to return to the "ghost ship" alone for some forgotten chore. It was an experience he'll never forget, he'll tell you.

"It was almost indescribable . . . that black pall of silence looming over the deserted pier. In the utter aloneness of the night, the drydocks are heart-chilling. Row upon row of black ships hunch their hulks against the sky. Once on board, it was as though I had stepped into another world or into the past, and I had to struggle for breath." He pauses from a feeling of remembered chill, then goes on: "You're alone in that dreadful quiet with only your own footsteps to suggest any living world."

It all adds up, say the believers, to one thing. The Sullivan boys come back in restless shapes and sounds to remind the world of that dark day in '42. It was a bloody battle, they mean to say, but not a useless one. They accomplished their mission. Henderson Field was saved.

Historians support this message. In their "Battle Report," a book published over 20 years ago, authors Walker Karig and Eric Burdon stated in regards to the naval battle at Guadalcanal: ". . . in the end, mistakes were cancelled out by valor. Let none deny praise to those who fell that bloody night. . . ."

The five Sullivans, it is said, come back to claim that rightful praise for Admiral Callahan and his hard-fighting van who all lie today in that sea of dead ships . . . Ironbottom Sound.

What better messenger than the "dead" ship named in their honor? Will it be a modern "FLYING DUTCHMAN?" That phantom vessel has been written up countless times and forms the basis of Wagner's opera, "Der Fliegende Hollander." Sailors for centuries have told of seeing the FLYING DUTCHMAN, a full-rigged ship at sea, doomed to sail forever because of the captain's spirit that will not rest. Is the U.S.S. THE SULLIVANS with its disquieted Sullivans-crew fast becoming the specter ship of the twentieth century?

The Giant Specter

Today as one walks through the township of Horsham, Pennsylvania, one sees highways and byways crossing and recrossing his pathway. Frequently his steps pass busy shopping centers filled with the bustle of cars grating in and out of tight parking lines. The air is filled with the sounds of screeching children, noisy horns and the glaring lights of store signs announcing their identities.

It was not always so.

About a century ago this area surrounded a gloom-rested hill that arose in the wooded sections north of Willow Grove. It was a well-known area traversed by stage coaches all through the 18th and 19th centuries. So many stage coach horses lost their lives along that perilous stage line that the woods above Willow Grove became strewn with the carcasses of the unfortunate beasts. The hilltop finally became so identified as the horses' final resting place it was known as "Horseheaven". Finally the name became shortened to "Horsham."

In spite of the gaunt skeletons stabbing into the moss-coated ground, the tree-packed hills above Willow Grove were beautiful in the spring. The lush green of all things growing was sweet of scent and inviting. Scurrying opossums crackled past the violet-picker and scarlet tanagers broke swiftly across his path.

But in the late autumn Horseheaven was a different matter. Few, if any, dared venture for a walk in the woods at that time when owls hooted overhead and weasels slithered into hidden holes.

It wasn't just because of the early dark, the numbing frost or the shriek of owls that walkers denied themselves the woods above Willow Grove. It was because of the Giant Specter.

The Giant Specter had earned a fearsome reputation in that region. He had stalked many a woodsman or bird-watcher with his huge footsteps plunging eerily through the dry twigs of the forest floor. Sometimes the Specter preyed upon an individual — a hunter or farmer cutting a short path through the woods; other times he followed a whole group hurrying home from a church meeting or a barn-raising. In every case he was described by the witnesses in the same manner.

The Giant was an enormous shapeless being that appeared suddenly from a clump of trees charging at a fierce pace. He often swung into a circle about the traveler, almost touching his body, but not quite. Then with a terrible roar like a winter gale, he would lunge sideways and disappear into the wooded area opposite.

Everyone agreed he was about 12 to 15 feet in height. His manner, it was said by witnesses, varied at times. Occasionally he sauntered at a moderate pace. More frequently he charged at high speed. Sometimes he pursued. Sometimes he swished like an icy draught in front of the walker and preceded him as he ran. In every instance, he was overpoweringly big and fearsomely noisy. And he appeared only in the chilly days and dusks of late autumn.

For nearly two centuries he held awesome reign over Horseheaven Hill. Then as the area grew in population and homes and roads filled the dark recesses of the formerly wooded section and the trees vanished under the woodsmen's axes, the Giant Specter was seen less and less.

It has been suggested that the ghostly, loud-stepping giant was a cluster of dry rustling leaves swept up from the woods' floor into a whirling mass that ran at the will of the winds. Such an explanation demands many identical repeat performances throughout the centuries by a most creative wind. Would this be possible?

Every legend-loving, ghost-geared teller of tales knows that it is not.

At any rate, the Giant Specter and the ghostly carcasses and the wind-haunted woods of Horseheaven are forever gone and the lonely walker is safe again.

The Odd Ghosts of Ottsville

Dr. Richard Blasband, the eminent psychiatrist, and his attractive wife, Inge, live with their young daughter on a beautiful hillside in Ottsville, Pennsylvania. Their home is a picturesque old stone structure that they have graced with simple decorative taste ranging from Early American to modern Danish.

There is also an unforseen addition to the house that they had not counted on when they bought it . . . ghosts.

Inge Blasband with a vigorous shake of her pretty blonde head, comments, "Whoever they are, they are here."

"They?" she is asked.

"Yes, a talkative man and woman. My husband and I had heard strange voices at different times and in different areas of the house from the very day we moved in a few years ago. But neither of us mentioned it. It all seemed too ridiculous. Then one day something happened that made us pay attention to this strange phenomenon."

"What was that?", she is questioned.

"We let friends of ours from New York spend their vacation here while we were away on our vacation. They're old friends and very down-to-earth people. When we came back they had an eerie story to tell us.

"It seems, just as we had, the two began hearing voices in the house the very first day. Like us also, they didn't mention it to each other, it semed so silly. Finally, at the dinner table that first night, one of them remarked about hearing a voice calling, then a conversation between a man and a woman. The other hastily added that he, too, had heard such talking. They agreed on their experiences — they were identical. First there was the sound of a voice calling someone. Then followed a conversation between a man and a woman. The words were soft at first, then grew to an excited pitch until finally there came the sound of a door slamming, then dead silence.

"The couple searched the house the next day. They found nothing.

"In the afternoon, the husband decided to look over the old carriage house on the property. He was admiring the worn stout beams overhead when suddenly he heard two people talking. Obviously a man and a woman. The exact sentences were indistinguishable, but the voices were clear. Then, as had been the case the day before, the sounds rose in a crescendo of excitement as though a heated argument were going on. Then followed the loud slamming of a door and complete quiet. The husband looked all about him. Of course, there was no one."

Dick Blasband nods as Inge recounts their friends' strange visit. "By the time we heard the story from them we realized we, too, had tales to exchange. We admitted to our friends, and to each other, for the first time, that we had a house with a phenomenon . . . a talkative ghost couple."

Dick leans back in his study chair and adds an interesting note. "The four of us discussed a fascinating part of the voices. They spoke in old-fashioned words . . . talk of a century or so ago. Obviously not speech as we hear it today."

"That's not the end of the story, either," adds Inge. "As the four of us sat in the front room talking about the experience, we suddenly heard a clock chiming the hour. The notes were deep and unmistakably the brassy sound of a clock's chimes.

"We stopped talking. The wife looked over at me and said, 'Those are beautiful chimes. We heard them while you were away but were never able to find where the clock was . . .'

" 'How could you?' I answered, exchanging amazed glances with Dick. 'We have no chiming clock.' "

Inge brushes her hair with one hand, thoughtfully. "Dick and I hear those chimes still — every now and then."

"We also hear someone calling on many occasions," adds Dick. "Sometimes I'm out in the garden and I think I hear Inge calling me or she's in the kitchen and thinks I've been calling her. We frequently think we hear the other calling."

Inge contributes another strange experience that happened when a friend of Dick's was visiting them. "In the middle of the night the young man heard footsteps slowly coming up the stairs. He knew it could not be anyone at that hour. Yet he felt it had to be. He turned cold as he lay there waiting. Finally there was silence. The footsteps had ceased. Of course, the next day, he learned, as he suspected, it was no one of us."

So the life of the Blasbands goes on in their Ottsville house, so strangely permeated with voices from the past. Who is the conversational couple? Were they occupants of the place many, many years ago? Did they argue a great deal about something? Do their conflicting thoughts and spirited words still hover in the atmosphere of their old home?

Inge and Dick Blasband are hoping someday they will know the answers to all these questions.

The Ghostly Guests in a Langhorne Farmhouse

The Robert Messingers of Old Lincoln Highway in Langhorne, Pennsylvania, have a strange tale to tell. They insist their house is haunted.

Puzzling events have been occurring ever since they moved into the 18th Century stone house in 1961.

The first of a long run of strange and often frightening incidents came the first week they occupied the house. In the middle of the night Nancy Messinger awoke suddenly. The room was filled with the odor of strong tobacco smoke. Since her husband didn't smoke, the surprising experience kept her awake the rest of the night.

Robert Messinger dismissed the story the next day. He felt Nancy was just over-tired from moving chores. They soon both forgot the incident.

But a few nights later it occurred again. This time it happened to Bob. As he was getting ready to retire, the scent of heavy pipe smoke floated into the bedroom. The hall was permeated with it. He checked the living room fireplace, the kitchen stove, the outside trash burners. Nothing burning anywhere.

Still the Messingers didn't worry too much. Perhaps his clothes from work carried the odor of smoke. . .

One Sunday morning a few weeks later a new scent pervaded the house: the toasty fragrance of baking bread. The two searched the downstairs. It came definitely from Bob's den, the former kitchen of the farmhouse. There was nothing in Nancy's kitchen cooking. Not even a neighbor was baking bread.

Not long afterwards a new puzzle entered the picture. Nancy was in the kitchen when she heard notes struck on the spinet piano in the living room. She looked into the room. It was empty.

These inexplicable phenomena soon multiplied. On evenings when the Messingers would go out and leave a table lamp burning in "dim" position, they'd return and find the switch on "bright." Or the lights entirely out and the house in darkness.

The parlor rocker frequently was found creaking back and forth when no one was near it. Lamp shades often quivered as though brushed by a passing person.

One memorable incident involved the grandmother clock in the living room. It chimed without ceasing. When the clock repairman arrived and unscrewed the back of the case he found the chain in the clockworks tied in 13 evenly-spaced knots. Later when the Messingers went on vacation and Bob removed the pendulum, they left the clock reading seven-thirty. Upon their return the hands pointed to eight o'clock.

The two most frightening experiences happened to Nancy. The first occurred when Bob had to leave a repair job on the front door unfinished in order to attend a meeting in town. He didn't have the time to put hinges or the doorknob on, so he nailed the door against the jamb.

Nancy sat sewing on the sofa while the children slept upstairs. Suddenly without warning the front door crashed inwards at her feet as though slammed by a powerful force. She stiffled a scream as she sat gaping at the open doorway. The nails which Bob had bent over firmly now stood straight out from the door jamb. Outside the night was still without a hint of wind.

The second occasion was a night when Bob was working in his den and Nancy was reading in the living room. She sat on the sofa facing the tiny stairway that wound upstairs. The children were asleep. Her head was bent over her book.

The clock chimed eleven. In the intense quiet that followed, she suddenly felt alerted. Her scalp tightened. There were distinct footsteps overhead!

Not light running ones, such as children make, but pounding ones as if from a man's weight.

Nancy stared at the foot of the stairway. Paralyzed, she listened to the footfalls descending. One by one they came nearer. She screamed out.

"Bob!"

The footsteps ceased. Bob appeared in the den doorway behind her. He bolted up the stairs and checked the entire second story. Nothing.

Such unnerving events have not diminished over the years. The Messingers claim that in spite of repeated attempts to unravel the mysteries of their house, they are beseiged by odors of smoke; scent of baking; lights going on and off; voices calling their names and the sound of a man humming in different rooms of the house.

The Messingers children, too, are involved. Bonnie frequently complains of hearing "someone in Bobby's room" at night. One Halloween she was so insistent that someone was going through her brother's Trick or Treat bag, her father came up, turned on the light and found Bobby's bag, which he had hung up high out of reach, on the floor with the candy and apples strewn about.

Young Bobby contributes one of the strangest aspects to the puzzle, according to Bob and Nancy. The child has a "friend" who visits him constantly.

On one occasion, an early Sunday morning, they found Bobby had been outside and picked grapes from the arbor. When questioned how he got out the bolted door, he said his "friend" had taken him out.

What does his friend look like? He has gray hair, a beard and he wears a high white collar and a black suit. Nancy Messinger has traced one of the owners of the house in the last century. He was a schoolteacher named Pierson

Mitchell. His picture in an old historical book shows a man with gray hair, a beard and a high white collar with a dark suit.

Other owners included a farmer, his wife and two daughters in the early years of this century. His name was James Gallagher. One daughter married and moved away; the other stayed at home. When buying the house, Nancy and Bob were told that the previous owners were going to move to another state. Later, they learned the family had moved only to a nearby town. Was there a reason? Were they, too, besieged?

The Messingers have spent time and money investigating the baffling phenomena which pursue them. First, friends were asked over to determine if unusual incidents would occur to them. The Messingers were not long in finding out.

Women friends of Nancy invited to a swim party that summer asked if Nancy's father lived with her. Nancy shook her head. "Why do you ask?"

"Because we heard a humming from the kitchen when we went in the house a moment ago."

Another time Bob invited a close friend over. They had no sooner sat down at the kitchen table to talk when a startling incident occurred. A plate flew off from the top of the breadbox and, just missing the friend's head, landed on the floor by the table.

"Musta been vibration from a passing truck," decided the guest. He got up, watched Bob replace the plate, as it was, flat on the breadbox.

Testing, Bob nudged the plate forward and caught it as it fell downward. Logical. That's the way a plate would fall. The men returned to the table. "Strange," said the friend, "how that coulda flown straight out and across the room—"

He was interrupted by the whirring sound of the plate flying at right angles across the kitchen again, missing his head by inches.

That friend still scratches his head over the inexplicable event. What caused that plate to fly off the breadbox? What has caused all the weird phenomena?

The Messingers are searching desperately for answers. An electrician has looked at the fuse box and checked the electrical circuits. Nothing amiss.

A building contractor has looked at the foundation of the house. It is firm without a sign of shifting or new settling. Intensive searching of the premises has never revealed a sign of field mice, loose boards nor underground disturbances.

Bob has cut away all touching tree branches and ruled out the possibility of any reflections from window glass.

Yet the strange guests continue to come.

"There is only one conclusion we can come to," says Robert Messinger reluctantly. "We are haunted."

In spite of everything, the Messingers love their home in Langhorne. They refuse to be put out of it by ghosts.

They will continue to live there with this strangest of tales to tell.

Christmas Eve at Pen Rhyn

Abraham Bickley looked proudly about him. His great room, aglow with crackling fire and sputtering tapers, pleased him. "Pen Rhyn", as he called his estate on the Delaware, reflected him in every respect. His handsome brick house, his full stable, his comfortable dining board . . . all bespoke the success of this Welshman, as they had since the day he bought the place in the 1740's.

Now on Christmas Eve, it was a good thing to feel contentment and a little measure of pride, but —

Abraham turned and gazed into the blazing hearth. He clasped his hands behind him and grunted a half-spoken oath. The truth was, this was not a happy Christmas Eve. He had just quarreled with Robert and a father could not entirely overlook words with a son in such a hallowed hour, not even with a worthless son —

The December wind knocked against a window shutter and slammed an uneasy disturbance into the room. Mr. Bickley looked over at the window. Poor account and ungrateful son that Robert was, he didn't like the idea that the boy had dashed from the room a few minutes ago and out the front door with such unreasoning fervor. What if he had chastized Robert for marrying a girl so unsuitable for a Bickley, so opposite of what he, Abraham, had planned for his son — was that cause for a boy to curse his father, his family name, his centuries of tradition and stamp from the house . . . all on this hallowed Christmas Eve, to add indignity to family dishonor?

Abraham walked slowly toward the window overlooking the river and peered out the wavering hand blown glass panes. Why wasn't Robert back again, walking into the house this minute, apologizing?

Mr. Bickley grunted and turned away from the window. The truth was, he knew in his heart, the boy wouldn't be back. Wasn't he a Bickley, headstrong as the old Welshman himself? And, in truth, hadn't Abraham ordered the boy out and told him never to return? Ah — sometimes it didn't pay to be a wall of a Welshman.

A knock on the heavy oak panels of the front door aroused Abraham. He hurried to open it. There was no one there. Only the ice-fisted wind. With a sense of uneasiness Abraham closed the door.

He never opened it with ease on a Christmas Eve again.

Nor did anyone else for many Christmas Eves to come through subsequent centuries, for that night a ghost was born for lovely Pen Rhyn on the Delaware.

Robert Bickley did indeed leave his estate that night and never return. He had, according to the story that has lain within the walls of Pen Rhyn for hundreds of years, dashed out of the house with curses on his father's name, and plunged himself into the ice-packed Delaware. He was never seen again.

Until Christmas Eve, that is.

On that night each year, the old tale goes, he arises out of the frozen river and comes up to the front door of Pen Rhyn and pounds on the door panels. When the door is opened he stands before the person, his worn silk coat soaked and covered with river slime, water dripping in frozen droplets from the lace at his wrists and throat, his mouth frozen in a curse and his whole body weaving in moans.

When the front door slams shut before this vision of horror, he moves deliberately toward a window, then another, tapping for admittance on the icy panes until he has struck on each and every one.

Inside the fright-filled house, Pen Rhyn's inhabitants are said to have reported that upon the stroke of midnight eerie cries sweep the house from the first floor to the top story. When the clocks cease to chime, the shrill cries stop and the loud knockings and rappings of the ghost of Robert Bickley vanish for good.

Until the next Christmas Eve.

Today Pen Rhyn of Andalusia stands bold in yellow stucco alongside the flowing Delaware, seemingly quite unaware of its blood-stirring ghostly visitor. It is a school at the present time and is filled only with the bell-like laughter of the carefree young.

Even centuries of dripping, moaning ghosts will have a difficult time drowning out such laughter — still . . . .

Can we be sure?

It isn't Christmas Eve again . . . just yet.

Last Revel in Printz Hall

"Aye, good Quaker, you have a faithful heart but not much that's stout in it, iffen you ask me," taunted the musician, Peter Matthews, as he took a draught of ale and slammed his feet into the midst of the old Chester tavern, snapping his fiddle to his chin.

Quaker Quidd wagged a hand in the direction of the bobbing form of the musician as the rest of the tavern guests howled and stamped their feet to the lilting rhythms.

"I ask thee, how stout is *thy* heart, Peter Matthews?," called out the Quaker with persistence. "I wager thee a good silver coin thee could not spend one night in my tenant house after dark! No more than I nor any other man!"

Peter ceased fiddling and gave a hop back towards the table where the older man sat.

"I'll take that wager, Master Quidd! The easiest coin I ever be earning. I've sung for my supper and played for my straw pallet on many an eve, but I never was paid to make my bed with ghosts from out the woodwork!"

With those words accompanied by a round of laughter from every corner of the old Chester tavern, Matthews packed his faithful violin into its hempen case and leaped like a hart after the pouncing form of Master Quidd as he plunged out the door.

The Quaker pulled his wide-brimmed hat down close over his eyes and bent his head against the autumn evening's wind.

"Thee hops merrily to the tunes in thy head now, fancy fiddler, but wait until thee sees my ghost-gnawed tenant house. I warrant then thy bones alone in thy thin skin shall do the dancing as thee shakes and quakes to the Devil's tune!"

Peter was jumping over a branch fallen across the road and seemed scarcely to hear the other's continuous rambling.

The Quaker was still chattering as he led the way into an overgrown area of thicket and brambles. He was telling the musician of the long ago past when this old house had served as the home of the first Governor of New Sweden back in 1644, years before William Penn set foot on the shore of this new land.

"The Royal Swedish Governor was named Johann Printz and a less popular fellow never lived in the environs of Chester, I assure thee, fiddler. Printz was vain and wordly in ways with not a thought for the good of his colony but only for the substance of his coffers. He lasted only a few years and was recalled to Sweden leaving his Printz Hall empty of gold and jewels and silver-buckled feet dancing over its waxen floors till the early hours of the morn."

Peter gave a skip and started to sing.

"I care not for the golden thing,
  I live only to dance and sing!"

Quaker Quidd stopped still in his tracks and turned to stare at the younger man.

"Peter Matthews," he said with a clicking of his tongue, "sometimes methinks thee is no larger brained than the chickens in my back yard. Come on now, a moment only and thee will see Printz Hall."

Peter paused for a second as the outline of a large building loomed over them suddenly in the fretting light of a pale moon that tried to peer out from behind black clouds.

"Here be thy home for the night, fiddler," murmured Quaker Quidd with a tone of satisfaction in his voice. "Here will thee earn the hardest-won coin of thy life." Quidd turned and stared at the slim figure behind him. "I have spent a night here. I know whereof I speak. By tomorrow, so shall thee."

Matthews thrust his head forward through the darkness to get a good look.

"Appears to me to be quiet enough a spot for my tired bones," commented the musician whose voice wavered slightly more at this point.

The night breeze swished a dry branch against his cheek as he looked over at the Quaker. Quidd was nodding knowingly.

"Sleep well with the Governor, good fiddler," the older man said and he patted the musician on the back reassuringly. With a swing of the lantern in one hand and a salute from the other, the Quaker with his glimmering light pulled away in the dark.

Peter Matthews shrugged off a sense of loneliness and started whistling as he pushed through tall weeds towards the front door. Once there, he leaned against the rotting timbers of the great oak expanse and listened as it gave way with a woeful creak.

He hesitated, then turned and looked over one shoulder. A faint gleam from the other side of the thicket showed him the Quaker was watching from a distance.

With a heave, Peter pushed open the door wide and walked inside.

The odors of closed-in air, rotting pine and rain-soaked tapestries were almost overwhelming. Peter swallowed hard and laid his fiddle down against a carved chair while he fumbled to find a flint box on the fireplace mantel and the remnant of a taper in a candle box half chewed apart by rats.

He lit the remains of a fat candle and looked about him. Blue tiles framing the fireplace shone back at him bright as the day they'd first been fired. On a wall opposite, a row of oil portraits gleamed faintly in the darkness. Stern-eyed cavaliers in their rich velvets and lace cuffs looked down at him.

"Good evening, gentlemen," said Peter with a low bow. "We'd best meet since we shall be spending the night together in this cobwebbed palace. I am Peter Matthews, the fiddler of Chester, the merriest fiddler in the colony. If the night proves too dull for such fine cavaliers as yourselves, pray tell me so that I may lighten your boredom with a lovely concert."

Peter pulled a network of sticky spider webs from the top of his head as he poked around the fireplace gathering some remnants of pine knots and splinters of sticks. In the next minute he had a small fire sputtering in the great hearth. He stretched out on the dust-coated rug for his night's sleep.

Hugging his arms to his body for as much warmth as possible, he closed his eyes and tried to get his thoughts centered on the happy lot of the caterpillar snug in a silken cocoon. A strange flapping sound startled his ears and he sat up. He lay back again, a smile on his lips. Bats. Bats were aloft in the rooms above. He'd heard them many a time before when he'd made his bed in the hay of a barn. No harm in that sound, he decided. Tonight even the company of bats was welcome.

Finally as the fire dimmed to ashes, his eyes became heavy and in spite of the chill, he fell asleep.

Suddenly he was awakened by he knew not what. All he knew was that he was awake and was wide awake as he'd ever been in his life. He listened. There was the roar of a night wind in the chimney and a slamming of tree limbs against window panes all over the house but he was sure now there was more than that. Much more.

He pulled up into a sitting position and waited.

There it was: a tread and a clank on the great stair in the hallway outside. Then in the doorway appeared a dark figure with steeple-crowned hat, black cloak, jack-boots, sword and corselet.

The terrified fiddler wanted to leap to his feet and jump out a window. He couldn't move.

The visitor started to speak. His voice rolled through the dark like thunder. "I am Johann Printz, Governor-general of His Majesty's American colonies and builder of this house. Arise, fiddler, I have need of thee. 'Tis the night of the autumnal equinox when my friends and I meet here for revel. Take thy fiddle and come! Speak not. He who would be my guest, must not utter a word. Only *I* command the voices of darkness!"

Whether he wished to or not, the fiddler knew he must obey the man before him. He got to his feet, grabbed his fiddle in its hempen case and followed the huge form out of the room.

With a cold feeling in the pit of his stomach, Peter followed the towering form upstairs and along corridors that rang to the specter's boot heels. It was no task to follow the Governor for though there was no lantern or taper near them a steady phosphorous glow hovered about the man like a ring of moistness about the moon.

Finally they came to an ancient reception room and as they entered, Peter was dazzled. The floor, heavily waxed, gleamed in the light of hundreds of tapers in glittering wall sconces. Great logs snapped in two large fireplaces at each end of the room. Their flames were eye-catching to Peter for they had not an orange glow in their crackling flames but burned bright blue. Peter could hardly get his breath for a strong odor that pervaded the entire hall. Sulphur! The scent of the Devil's presence! His first thought was to turn and run. But he couldn't. The Governor was staring directly at him and with a raised finger ordered, "Play!"

While Peter leaned over and removed his fiddle from its case, slowly figures from all sides came pouring into the room. They were beautifully gowned ladies and velvet-jacketed men in dress of a hundred years before. Their eyes that stared at Peter were gleaming and penetrating as rock crystal.

"Play!," commanded the Governor.

Peter swallowed hard and snapped the fiddle to his chin. Soon he was playing as he'd never played before. The tunes poured out from his fiddle and bow and his whole body swayed with the vibrancy of the music. Tunes filled the air that he'd never known before, songs from another era.

The couples were swinging about the room, skirts of satin fluttering in the heavy air; the men's powdered wigs catching the taperglow like patches of moonlight.

After Peter knew not how long, the doors at the far end of the room opened and two henchmen struggled in bearing a large coffer

The guests stopped dancing as the tunes ceased and everyone turned and faced Peter, for the Governor was addressing him.

"You have performed well, fiddler. Now I shall reward thee for your well-kept silence as well as your fingers' skill." The Governor clapped his hands and at the signal the two henchmen raised the coffer's lid.

Gold! Heaps and heaps of gold flickered and sparkled into Peter's eyes like bright sunlight on a church chalice! Never did the fiddler think gold was so beautiful or so important. Suddenly he knew it was all that and more!

"Come, fiddler," urged the Governor. "Bring hence your fiddle's bag and let us fill it to the top, but remember well, not a word may you speak."

With a silent leap, Peter had his fiddle bag open and he poured in the gold until his arms ached. With it brimming to the top, he kicked along the fiddle itself and dragged the case as though it were a sack of golden flour out of the room and into the hall where the polished stairway beckoned him to the sweet outdoors and a new life as the richest man in the colony.

"Farewell, fiddler," the voices behind him called and he smelled the sulphur stronger than ever. What matter, thought Peter, the world was a new place to him now. He dragged the case slowly down the steps, breathing harder with each step. Finally he was at the bottom and as he reached for the big oaken front door he could not suppress his ardor another moment. A thought spun into his head that made him want to bounce with joy:

"Wait till I show this to old Quaker Quidd!," he shouted.

No sooner had he spoken than he heard wild laughter from the room at the top of stairs. Then he felt cobwebs begin to form about his face and the fiddle bag became light as paper in his grasp. Overhead the laughter ceased and all he could hear was the flapping of the wings of trapped bats.

He looked down. A smashed fiddle was at his feet; an empty case in his hand.

Peter gave a howl of pain and collapsed.

Nothing more could he remember until someone shook his arm. The sun was pouring in through the broken panes of the hall windows. He was lying on the floor by the front door.

"I see thee survived, good fiddler, even if thy fiddle did not.'

It was Quidd.

Peter looked at his instrument beside him. It lay in splinters. The hempen case was a crumpled heap. He clutched quickly at it. It was empty.

"Feel not too bad, musician. Thee must have trampled thy fiddle to death in fearful fright but thee still has something to show for thy brave though foolish spirits. Here!"

The Quaker dropped a silver coin into the empty fiddle case. "There's very little in life we experience, good friend, that does not reward us somehow."

Peter Matthews got to his feet and nodded. He had played a tune for the wildest dance of his life. He had played for a fiend and a fortune and lost both — fortunately. For was not this life, after all, with his ale and friends and happy tunes much the best? With this one silver coin he'd get himself a new instrument and continue where he'd left off in the old Chester tavern.

Not a word did Peter say to his Quaker friend about the night before. A man who'd been so sorely tempted was better off without telling details.

In Chester tavern that night a boy ran in with startling news. Old Printz Hall had just burned down to the ground. Peter gave an extra shake of his head as he fiddled gaily away. The spirits of Printz Hall had set the place on fire and he knew where they'd brought their coals from.

A Haunted Corner of Earth

"In this corner of earth have been the happiest moments of my life." So reads an inscription over the fireplace of an old home in Phillips' Mill on the Delaware River. Who put those words there? A charming schoolteacher of Miss Holmquist's School for Girls. Her name was Miss Shearman. She was a direct descendant of James Logan. She lived in this house which once served as the academic building for the school, taught there for many years, and finally made it her home.

Even though she passed away some years ago at an age well up into the nineties, she has continued to make it her home — according to the experiences of the house's recent residents, Nancy and Robert Brownstone.

"I never believed in ghosts," Nancy Brownstone told me with a wrinkle of her pretty brow, "but this house has changed my mind. Miss Shearman is still here. I can feel it in a thousand ways". Nancy sat down opposite me. The cool dark room around us grew more sombre as the sun set outside. Oak beams and carved woodwork gave the room the cast of buckwheat honey. A strange quietness settled about us as a soft wind rustled the leaves against the window screens.

"See this fireplace with its carved motto?" I followed Nancy gaze at the inscription looking down upon us. "Miss Shearman carved that. She was a wood carver, as well as a teacher and a famous hostess. She used to pour tea by this fireside every afternoon. They say notables, artists, diplomats — many people sat here where we are now, sharing tea with Miss Shearman."

I nodded wonderingly, knowing a strange story was to unfold.

"When we first moved in a few months ago," continued Nancy, "I sat down one chilly afternoon right here for a moment's rest. I began to feel I was visiting at one of Miss Shearman's teas. I could feel she was there. I could just see a group of people sitting by the fire. I looked into the big fireplace where cold ashes piled in gray unawareness of a later winter cold. I began to imagine how warm and friendly it must be in that room with a fire going. For me, a New York apartment girl who knew nothing of how to start a fire or of having the privilege of sitting close to one for a spot of tea, the whole picture was enchanting. I sat back glowing in the thought."

My gaze rested first upon the cold emptiness of the fireplace at that moment, then on Nancy's thoughtful face. "Go on," I urged.

"Suddenly," she continued, "as I was gazing into the fireplace, a fire sprang to life! Out of dead ashes a roaring fire blazed up! I could hardly believe my eyes!" Nancy looked straight at me. "It was uncanny. When Robert came home later that evening, it was still blazing."

I could only nod my head in awe.

"Also, one night as my husband and I were sitting here we heard the boards of the upstairs floor creaking. I went up, as we knew no-one was up there but our little girl who should be fast asleep in her crib. I investigated. She was. But it was a strange thing. Over in one corner of her room a stack of metal rods had been piled up. We had intended soon to place them back in the proper windows. When I looked into our little girl's room, the rods were in the crib with her!"

"Just last night," smiled Nancy, "we had another odd occurrence. My husband said something about the possibility of changing an aspect of the house. I told him he better not — Miss Shearman might not approve and he'd be in for it! Just as I finished speaking a glass globe around a light fixture suddenly and unexplainedly exploded. The shattering sound was quite unnerving."

I replied that I should well imagine so. It was easy to see Miss Shearman was an alert ghost. Knew everything that was going on!

"I should say so," Nancy nodded. "You know Miss Shearman had a habit everyone in the village here associated with her. She used to call to any passing friend, "Yoo-Hoo!" Many times my two neighbors mentioned how nice it was when they'd go in their back gardens to hear the shrill call of white-haired Miss Shearman from out of her bedroom window, "Yoo-Hoo!" They quite miss it with her gone this spring. She used to love to lean out of her window and watch her friends appear and disappear below."

Nancy continued as her gaze followed mine to the outside garden. "I was outside gardening this spring when I heard the sound of my next door neighbor arriving back from a vacation. I heard her front door slam and the back door open up to let in the spring air. Then it came, clear as any sound I ever heard— "Yoo-Hoo!", right from the upstairs window. It came from the room where Miss Shearman had spent the closing months of her life, and from where she called to so many neighbors. Even though it was a warm spring day," Nancy said, "I shivered."

I got up to go, looking about me expectantly. There was nothing but the tiny elevator with its listless ropes, (which Nancy told me they'd leave on one floor and find later on another), the muted browns of the old woodwork, the alive touches of Nancy and Robert's hand-made tapestries on the walls and half-done on easels.

But Miss Shearman was there, too. I could feel it. I could even understand her reluctance to leave such a meaningful spot. Her carved words over the fireplace were the last remembrance I have of my "tea hour" in her home — in her own private "corner of earth."

The Inn-Place for Haunters

When Carl Lutz bought the old Logan Inn in New Hope a few years ago, he found he owned not just an historical building but a legend. Not long after that he discovered he housed a score of inexplicable phenomena as well.

The Logan Inn was originally the local tavern of Coryell's Ferry, the main crossing of the Delaware River above Trenton before, during and after the Revolution. Located on the much-used stagecoach route between Philadelphia and New York the hostelry was a popular place. It was called in those days simply, "The Ferry Tavern."

The inn was heavily frequented during the War of Independence and must have throbbed to the rafters when General Washington's men were quartered there and made wassail that Christmas time of 1776, drinking to the success of their cause and the downfall of King George the Third in his American colonies.

After the war years the inn continued to be the focal point in the life of the townspeople for they gathered there to quaff ale and exchange the news of the day. One time around 1790 this news was high disaster for the village — a whole complex of mills located there burned down to the ground.

As the town recouped from the loss and the mills were rebuilt, the village changed its name from "Coryell's Ferry" to "New Hope" . . . the name it bears to this day.

The inn, however, retained its same name until well into the 19th century. Then in 1829 its owner, a Mr. Steele, sold it to the village's oldest resident, Abraham D. Meyers. The incoming landlord dubbed his tavern a new nomen indigenous to the area — the name of Logan. He called it, "The Logan House."

The historical background that intrigued Mr. Meyers was the incident in which William Penn's secretary, James Logan, wishing to express his brotherhood with the Indians, exchanged names with a Lenni-Lenape chief. He took the Indian's name for his own and gave his illustrious "James Logan" to the chieftain.

In commemoration of this friendly act and as a unique hallmark, so to speak, for the inn, Meyers commissioned a local craftsman, Samuel Cooper to create a large weathervane in the form of the Indian Logan. Cooper worked it out of sheet metal and mounted the image on a 40 foot pole in front of the tavern.

All went well for the great chieftain for over a hundred years. Then one night in the mid-years of this century the pole suddenly broke and the inn's owner stashed it away in the barn at the rear of the property.

That night (and it was February 22nd, the anniversary of the birth of Mr. Coryell's great Revolutionary friend, George Washington) a fire broke out in the barn and nearly everything was destroyed. On that night also was born the legend that if one moved the Indian from his accustomed place, fire would break out!

The durable chieftain then was placed on a post a few feet tall in front of the inn once more, the post being considered a reasonable substitute for the old pole.

Carl Lutz, though, did not consider it a fair exchange. He decided the metal figure should rest imposingly on a 40 foot pole as it originally did. Cautiously, he ordered the sign re-instated on a tall pole overlooking the inn's lawn. As the order was carried out he noticed it was February 22nd, 1971!

"I was not cowed by that realization," says Carl Lutz. "I was putting him back where he belonged. I knew he could only be pleased by that!"

"As if to confirm Logan's pleasure with this act," notes Carl with amusement and satisfaction, "it rained on Washington's birthday and for five consecutive days afterwards! Assurance for us that there would be no fire!"

But more spirits than Logan's inhabit the old inn, Carl will tell you, and these seem largely to be family associations.

"Here are my grandmother and grandfather," says Carl, pointing up to an enormous oil portrait of his ancestors overlooking their richly carved furnishings filling the inn's hallway. Their aristocratic features gaze out at you. They seem confident of their dominance there. "I feel sometimes," adds Carl, gazing thoughtfully up at them, "that they really are here."

The owner sweeps the air with one hand. "For example, on numerous occasions and in nearly every room of the inn, I catch the scent of my grandmother's favorite fragrance — lavender. She and my mother used to buy the dried flowers and leaves and tie them into sachet packets for use in our drawers and closets. I often pick up that old familiar scent that I used to smell in her home as a child right here in the inn.

"My mother, too, feels the presence of her mother here with us," continues Carl. "Not so long ago she had an unusual experience for which she has no other explanation than the thought that her mother was looking after her and helping her.

"Mother had dinner at the home of a friend one evening. She wore a garnet cross on a chain about her neck — a family heirloom that means much to her sentimentally. When she returned home she found the necklace gone. We called the hostess and we all searched but none of us could turn up the treasured piece. The next morning when my mother awoke she saw something glimmering across an armchair near the head of her bed. She looked closely and found that the cross and chain hung carefully from the arm of a chair. No one had put it there!

Another unique experience occurred at the time Carl was first settling down into the new business. It concerned a Witch's Ball.

A friend of Carl's had gone up and down all day from the dirt basement to the upstairs helping to clean up and sort out. Suddenly, on one particular trip down into the cellar his eyes spotted an object resting in the center of the path he'd been traversing all day long. It was a beautiful glass globe of a soft peach tint. It glowed up at him from the dirt floor.

Amazed that such a fragile item should be whole and intact in the midst of such disarray, the friend gently picked up the glass ball and placed it on a base inside a cabinet behind the inn's bar.

Carl examined it carefully and decided it could be only one thing: a Witch's ball — the charm used by superstitious people in the old days to ward off evil spells and hexes. The globes were usually hung in nets by a door or in a window or displayed as the inn owners were doing on a base of some sort.

Then one day, just as mysteriously as it appeared, it disappeared. The pale peach globe vanished and has never been seen since.

The inn has been filled with other wonders beyond this, Carl can tell you. A stout chain kept across the foot of the inn's stairs has often been heard to clank and crash again the wall as though suddenly released for some person's passage. When the owner checks almost instaneously, he finds it still in place as though untouched. Tiny bulbs in a chandelier over the bar have been loosened when no human hand was near it. A locked door upstairs opens repeatedly, seemingly by itself. In the tavern room where a fire is lit in the old fireplace, it behaves as erratically as a prima donna. One minute it burns furiously and in the next dims to a few ashes, only to spurt into wild life in the next instant!

"It's all fantastic," muses Carl. "But no phenomena surpasses the strange incident that occurred in the kitchen one day.

"I was most put-out one afternoon," recalls Carl, "to find that no one in the kitchen had prepared a supply of melba toast for the dinner hour. Now that is one of the features here at the inn — our garlic-buttered melba toast. I held out the empty bowl that should have been filled with the crusty slices and inquired why no one had fixed a fresh supply. Everyone seemed much chagrined. They had all, curiously, overlooked that one daily routine.

"I was in no mood for excuses. I was displeased and stalked out. Obviously, I had to content myself with the unhappy realization that no guest at the inn that evening would get melba toast.

"Sometime later I went into the kitchen and my eyes fell again on the melba toast bowl. I nearly keeled over. It was filled to the brim! Each piece was carefuly toasted and buttered as usual, except for one strange fact — each was toasted on only one side. I asked about. Who had so deftly and neatly made up the fresh supply? No one knew anything about it and seemed as astonished as I. Not a soul had been near that bowl! It seems my melba toast had been prepared by some well-meaning but inexperienced spirit cook!"

The inn stands as one of New Hope's most historic buildings as well as one of its most popular dinner spots. Its Victorian dining room with its glow of ruby lamps and velvety red walls are inducive to the most pleasant of dining. Its mellow-toned bar is the favorite meeting place of numerous residents and visitors to the town.

It also houses the Lutz family and a host of ghostly-doings.

"It's a strange home, but we love it," Carl concludes. "None of us feels unhappy because of these presences here. We feel comfortable with them and think they are comfortable with us. We all agree they are friendly and want to look after us. They'll always be welcome."

Perhaps some dinner hour as you sit by the centuries-old window under the rafters that roofed the heads of Washington's men, you, too, will feel the presence of some other-world form. Or even of Chief Logan himself watching you from his Happy Hunting Ground!

The House with Things that Go Bump

It is not an uncommon-looking house. It stands in a perfectly normal area of the valley on Aquetong Road in New Hope. It sheltered a down-to-earth family, the John Loepers, a few years ago.

Yet, it is not an ordinary house as the family well remembers.

It all began not so many years ago when the family first moved into the house. The owner's wife, Jane, and his aunt together designed and made a set of hand-decorated curtains for the kitchen windows. The job was one they delighted in. The curtains would be colorful and different and the handiwork something they would pride themselves on for a long time.

The day the curtains were finished was a special one. The two women hung them carefully, then stepped back and admired the picture. They were perfect. The design of the precise stitching gave just the right homespun touch to the country airs of the kitchen. John was called in to add any complimentary comments he wished. He agreed. They were handsome.

He also made the remark that it was getting late and if they all still intended to knock off work for a while and take in a movie, they'd best be getting under way. Agreed. The three took off for a good show and a change of pace for the day.

Upon returning, Jane had to take another look at the freshly curtained windows. It was dusk. She swung into the kitchen and clicked on the light. Her hand remained poised in mid-air. She was gazing on an unbelievable sight.

Every one of the curtains was hanging in reverse. The design was against the window glass. The back side of the stitching hung frontwards.

This was impossible. She called her husband and he came into the room questioning. His jaw dropped open in disbelief.

"Am I imagining something?" she asked feebly.

He shook his head. "Nothing at all," he commented. "They were certainly hung right side out when we left!"

The two walked thoughtfully into the living room.

"Do you suppose we've got ghosts? Mischievous ones. You know, poltergeist?" asked Jane.

John gave a shake of his head. "No one could convince me that there's such a thing as ghosts. I'd have to have a doggoned good sign before I'd — "

At that precise moment a picture hanging on the wall crashed to the floor. Nothing broke. Just a reverberating sound filled the room.

The couple stared at each other. The husband quickly examined the wall and the picture hook on it. Everything was unchanged from what it was when he first hammered the hook into place. Neither the nail nor hook was loose, crooked or bent. He leaned over and picked up the picture. The frame was intact; the wire by which it hung was still in place, unbroken.

It was particularly strange, both noted, that the picture had fallen straight downward. An impossible feat, it would seem, since such a hook would necessitate the picture being lifted up and outwards from the wall to be released.

John had reached a point of complete vexation. "If there are ghosts in this house, let them give us another sign!"

He had hardly finished his sentence when straight down from the wall, a mirror crashed to the floor.

That ended all scepticism. "We've got ghosts," said John Loeper.

His wife couldn't agree more.

One evening some time later, after the couple had become more or less used to sharing their home with mischief-makers and noisy bumpers throughout the day and night, friends from Louisiana stopped in for a visit — a young man and his father.

The young friend sat in a big armchair and John and Jane flanked him, asking him questions that had been storing up for some time, since it had been quite a while since they had seen these Southern acquaintances.

The young guest's father sat on the sofa opposite them all. He placed his hat on the back of the couch and stretched his arms out lazily, relaxed and enjoying the conversation about him. Occasionally, John directed a question towards him, but for the most part, the young man did the talking.

Suddenly, John became aware that the father had arisen and gone behind the sofa. He came around again to the front with a smile. "My hat fell off. Just retrieving it. No bother."

The conversation went on. In a minute the hat slipped off the back of the couch again. The older man patiently got up, went around and picked it up again, hardly aware of his action, so engrossed was he in his son's story.

Less than five minutes later, the hat fell off again. The father got up, muttered sheepishly about the "fool hat" as he moved behind the sofa and bent over again. The others went on talking with such animation they scarcely noticed that it was a moment or two before the older man arose from behind the sofa and stood up. When he did so, a surprising thing happened.

With all joviality gone from his manner and his face pale as chalk dust, he motioned impatiently to his son.

"Come. We've got to be going!" Without another word and with his hat crushed unthinkingly against his chest, the older man bolted from the room and out the front door.

John and his wife stood up in amazement. The son, startled, mumbled quick apologies and followed his father out. In seconds the car ground out of the driveway and the guests were gone.

"Well!" breathed Jane.

"Hmm," murmured John. "What do you suppose was wrong with him?"

The next day they learned the answer. The son phoned to say he was sorry about their rude departure.

"It was Dad's hat," he explained. "Each time it fell off, as he thought, he replaced it securely on the back of the sofa. By the third time it disappeared, he was really puzzled. But when he went to grab it that last time, that was the end! He found himself engaged in a tug of war! The harder he pulled it up towards him, the harder *something* tugged it away from him. He finally got it with a wild snatch . . . but — Well, you can imagine how he felt. He thought his heart would stop from the shock!"

The John Loepers told the young friend they were sorry about the incident, but not surprised.

"We were haunted. Undeniably, nerve-shatteringly and fascinatingly haunted," says John today. "We don't talk about it much. People think you're an odd ball. But it's true. We were haunted and you know something? We wouldn't have missed the experience!"

Inn of Curiosity

"We're a place of curiosity," says Becky Brown, owner of the Phillips Mill Inn on the River Road a few miles above New Hope. "I don't know what it is, but people come in here unlike dinner guests arriving at any other restaurant. They seem in a state of . . . well, hushed expectancy. Yes, I think that's the way to describe it: hushed expectancy.

"I don't know whether it's the shadowy atmosphere in here — we're set well back off the terrace and garden — or whether it's the ghost stories that have been circulating, or just the oldness of the place — it was built in 1756 by Aaron Phillips. This was his barn. Of course, his mill was across the way (today the Phillips Mill Community Association) and his house was — and still is — the stone structure at the bend of the road. This building was just his barn but it's always had color and history to it somehow."

Becky's dark brown eyes look at you in flashes as she turns from the stove to the sideboard where she is dipping some pink veal tenders into a bed of moistened crumbs for one of the house's most delectable specialties, Veal Parmigiana.

"John and I — John Bell here — " she points to a young man who is busy stacking jars on a shelf — "without whom I couldn't manage — he's the indispensable partner! — and I feel this place has seen a lot happen within its walls. A lot of sadness, I think." Then as she pops the veal morsels into sizzling olive oil, "But we intend to break that hovering gloom — I don't know what else to call it — with a new air in here of cordiality and hearth-side warmth. Hard work rewarded with happy customers is bound to soften history with hospitality, don't you think?"

Judging from the rich scents welling up from the stove, a visitor could easily feel that this new air was already conjured up and doing well!

What has happened in the old house?

No one story that can be unearthed. The inn is a part of the same house that called forth the mysterious fires and unexplainable incidents for the Brownstones in their half of the house. It was during that same period of goings-on next door that the first recorded ghostly visitant appeared at the inn.

"I was walking up the stairs to the second floor in the inn," says a one-time resident there, "when suddenly a figure rounded the curve and started down towards me. She was dressed in a long black skirt and a white cambric waist with a high collar. Her hair was piled high in the fashion of the turn of the century. I stopped cold in my tracks, I was so stunned. The lady kept coming downwards and in a short time I felt the brush of her long skirts against my legs as she pushed calmly past. It was uncanny. When I turned and looked down after her, there was no one in sight. I quickly searched the first floor but I found nothing. It was the most eerie experience of my life. I don't believe in ghosts yet — well, I don't know how else to explain what happened."

The former tenant looks thoughtfully ahead. "Then there was a subsequent odd incident when I was staying there. "A young girl who was dining at the inn left her table and went upstairs to the powder room. When she came back down she looked at me with the strangest expression on her face. 'Who is the old-fashioned lady sitting in a rocker upstairs? She looks right out of a 1900's *Ladies' Home Journal!*'

"I just laughed but inside I was smiling knowingly. My friend was back again!"

It seems the old-fashioned lady has other tricks up her leg-of-mutton sleeves. She likes to create cold spots in the midst of a warm room or dash past a guest in a rush of cool air, or, as another former resident there reported, likes to start up or put out lights.

"Sometimes," says this inn occupant of a few years ago, "When I was upstairs I would smell the odor of kerosene and I'd check downstairs to find an old oil lamp on the hall table burning brisky away. It was a lamp I kept there only for atmosphere and possible emergency use. But during my stay there, I'd frequently find it lighted. In fact, I trained myself to keep alert for the scent of oil and go turn it off. Most often, after taking care of the situation downstairs, I'd return to the second floor to find an oil lamp there burning away and the electric lights I'd turned on all turned off!"

Today, John Bell smiles gently at the stories of the inn's old-fashioned lady. "We don't object to her being here. In fact, Becky and I would enjoy meeting her. She just won't show up for us, that's all."

Not so far, anyway," adds Becky as she stirs a simmering pot of Florentine Wedding Soup on the back burner. "But we have hopes — "

Did you say you've just bitten into some Boeuf a la Mode at your terrace-side table at the old Phillips Mill Inn and what? Your candle just blew out?

Have no fears, the old-fashioned lady just wants you to know you're not alone.

Teens in Terror

One summer not so long ago an incident occurred at a home not far from the center of New Hope. A 17-year-old boy and his girl friend were sitting beside his swimming pool. They had just been in for a last dip and were laughing and talking. All their friends had left and the boy's mother was back at the house preparing dinner. The young couple started to gather up their towels. Suddenly the air around them seemed unusually still. Even the rattle of dishes from the open kitchen door subsided. The last fingers of flesh-colored sunlight pulled at the horizon and then dropped out of sight. The boy and girl were alone.

The girl shivered and rubbed her arms. The boy leaned over to pick up a towel from the edge of the pool. His gaze was caught by something thick moving in front of him. A dampness brushed across his face. He felt rooted to the spot with an indescribable terror. He sensed that the girl had stopped rubbing her arms and was standing immobile also.

The two stared as though transfixed at a strange object moving along the edge of the pool. It was a pillar of thick white mist. It glided over the pool, then up and down in the water, then lifted up and dragged gently along the pool's edge. It swayed this way and that, as though dancing to some unheard rhythm.

The boy and girl dropped their towels and ran.

Back in the house, none of the family could make sense out of what the boy and girl had seen. But the young couple know what they saw and still recall it vividly. Both describe it as happening in precisely the same way.

Other teens have seen very special guests, too. One young man in the village has told his night terror. He was asleep in his room when he was awakened in the dead of night by a rustling sound coming from the corner of his room. He opened his eyes slowly, not sure but he was dreaming his feeling of uncertainty and fright. He heard the sound again. He sat up in bed uneasily. The full moon through his open window shattered the darkness with little spears of silver light. He could make out the outlines of the chairs and his chest of drawers in the half-light.

Then he saw it. A white shape with little form and of a substance at once both thick, yet also thin, like a cloud moved about his chest of drawers in the corner. The one clearly discernable feature to the spellbound boy was a head of hair. It was fiery red, set on top of a formless body of milky white substance.

The boy leaped from his bed and tore out of his room. He went outside and spent the night in wide-awakefulness sitting on the garden wall. He has never seen the sight again, but the memory of that night has never left him.

A college senior and his girl told me of their experience. They were sitting in an attic room in New Hope listening to records. Outside the night was black without a vestige of moon. They sat talking softly and staring into the flame of a lone candle in the room.

Suddenly the candle light lowered and went out. There was no sputtering or fluttering, no draft of air. It appeared to be smothered out of existence as if an unseen hand gently lowered itself down upon it. The two stopped talking. For a moment the sudden darkness startled them and they could not say a word.

As they sat motionless a strange thing happened. A shaft of light arose from behind the table where the candle had been burning. It slipped upwards along the wall, then glided across the room. It moved up and down, then sideways. It slipped down the attic stairs, then up again. The boy glanced out the window at the first appearance of the light believing it to be car lights from the road. There was nothing outside. Not a sign of a car headlight or the beam of a flashlight from some passer-by's hand. There was only dead blackness beyond the window.

It was a moving light similar to that ghost-gleam which haunts a famous manor house in England and which was photographed by a television camera not so long ago. In both cases the area where the lights appeared was untouched by any outside lights. No explanation in either case can be given.

One other case of a ghostly vision was told me by a young girl in Bristol township. She was visiting a friend in an old home just off Newburyport Road a few years ago. While her hostess was in the shower, the girl sat on her bed setting her hair. Suddenly she felt the presence of someone in the room. She looked up and there was the figure of a boy standing in the doorway. He stood perfectly motionless with his hands by his sides. His face was indistinguishable. His whole form was grey and not too clearly defined. After an instant the figure just vanished. The girl ran to her friend. Was her brother in the house? No, he was away. There was no-one else present but the mother downstairs and the two girls. This young girl will never forget her ghost-night, either.

So it is that young people in this Valley find as goodly a share of ghostly visitors as any English castle.

The Ghost of London Purchase

, Ten-year-old Sue Percival lay very still in her bed. The moon sent shivers of light into the room highlighting the arrow-straight bedposts and her dark chest of drawers, then rested in a gleaming pool in the doorway.

Sue kept her eyes fastened on the doorsill. It would be right there very soon that she would see him.

And he did come as he did every night. "He" was a friendly man who never ignored her as so many grownups did when they came calling. "He" would walk past with a proud air, look at her, smile gently and nod, then pass out her other door into the master bedroom beyond.

The repeated incident came to be a game. Sue looked forward to her guest each evening. She would lie in silence until very soon she'd hear his light steps coming up the back stairway which led up from the dining room below.

He was not a frightening visitor but a gracious one. He was dressed in a green coat that dipped to tails in the back with dark breeches beneath. His round tummy was covered with a waistcoat across which gleamed the gold chain of a timepiece.

Sue would watch the friendly little man pass through, then vanish through the doorway on the opposite side of her room. She would lie awake thinking about him for awhile (he was just someone who must live there, too, she decided); then she would turn over and go to sleep.

Mary Lou Percival, Sue's older sister, found the same gentleman a constant visitor also. She saw him almost every evening in the dining room as the family sat at dinner. Sue would see the identical figure in his green coat with waistcoat and breeches and fluttering wrist ruffles walk down the back stairs that descended from Sue's bedroom and pass behind the seated family at the dining room table, smiling as he walked. He seemed to signal Mary Lou with a courteous bow as though he were apologizing for intruding. He would circle the table then disappear up the stairway again.

This occurred in the summer of 1948. The Percivals were in a home they were renting for the summer from a family who were vacationing in Italy. The house was "London Purchase," a stone structure rising over green hillside stretches in Jericho Valley about four miles below New Hope. It was so named because it rested on land that was a grant from the king of England to William Penn and was later purchased by a land developing company in England called "The London Company."

Today the beautiful house still graces the countryside. Owned by the James J. O'Brien family, it stands out as a uniquely handsome home approached with a curve of driveway that circles the front entrance and on around back below the "old" part. That is the original section of the house which contains the "haunted" area according to Sue and Mary Lou.

Have Mr. and Mrs. O'Brien or their children met the kindly gentleman in the green coat and waistcoat? Not yet. But they are hopeful, they will tell you.

Sue today lives in Doylestown. She is Mrs. Peter Read. Mary Lou lives in Newtown Square and is Mrs. Peter Clauss. Both Sue and Mary Lou recall that strange summer very well. They remember the little courteous ghost with his misty aura and his pleasant manners vividly. They recall also the day the owners returned from Europe and asked first off, "Did you meet the friendly ghost of 'London Purchase?'" "

Mrs. Margaret Percival, the girls' mother who resides in Doylestown today, talks frequently of that mysterious summer of '48.

"All of us felt a presence in that house — in the old wing. Often I heard footsteps upstairs in the evening after I'd put the girls down. I'd be sure the children were walking around up there. When I would investigate, however, there was never anything.

"The girls were asleep in their beds in their rooms. All would be dead silence. Yet, I felt someone was there. We all felt it, but none of us were afraid. It was as though this presence were a part of the house and belonged there. If anyone was intruding, it was we!"

Possessed Possessions

Of all the ghosts I've tracked down in the Delaware Valley, none is so unique as those I classify as "Possessed Possessions."

Such hauntings are not ghostly houses, geographic areas or people. They are haunted objects. And they haunt whoever happens to own them.

A case in point is a cabinet that once belonged to Thom Street of Jenkintown in Montgomery County (see also his experience in "The Haunted House of Centennial Row" earlier in this book). Every night from the time he first obtained the piece of furniture, it kept him awake at night with loud bangings from the inside.

Thom would get up innumerable times and carefully examine the cabinet but could find nothing that would explain the rappings. He finally sold the piece to a man thinking that such a transfer should end its miseries. It didn't. A few days later the man called him up and asked what was with that cabinet? It kept him awake all night with loud knockings!

Thom thinks that eventually that man sold the piece of furniture to someone else. He guesses no one knows now just where or for whom the old cabinet is performing.

An antique dealer of Hunterdon County in New Jersey reports to me that he has haunted kitchen cabinets. He hears from time to time loud bangings from the interiors of his cabinets. As soon as he goes to investigate the noises cease.

The owner of a gift shop in New Hope told me recently of a troublesome papier-mache owl she once had in her place. She kept him on a shelf in a rear room. Whenever she walked into that area — Zoom!, right off the shelf he'd fly at her! Being of such a light substance, he never hurt her, but it was a startling habit — until she got used to it. Eventually, she was so accustomed to his antics, she'd go into the room, her arms extended like a half-back, poised to catch the bird.

One day a man bought it. She warned the customer of the creature's wayward ways. He seemed undaunted as he planned to use him as a decoy for hunting and not as a decorative touch in his home. A suitable fate, thought the shop owner, for the ornery owl.

Another resident of New Hope, a night club producer, is known to own a strangely possessed flip-top desk in his apartment. Loud rappings and knockings issue forth from its interior at the most unsuspecting times and to add to the startling performance, it occasionally sends its front leaf flying open. None of which seems to have provoked the patient owner into parting with the piece.

Also in Bucks County, I heard of a movie studio that was plagued with telephone-teasings. Frequently, the phones would ring or their array of extension lights flash when no one was on the line or in the room. Today the place appears deserted. Were the "phoney phones" the reason? I haven't been able to locate anyone there to give an answer.

Victor Barger of Philadelphia told me a few years ago of the oddest "possessed possession" I ever heard of before or since. An aged Negro woman who lived near him when he was a boy owned a glass vase that was unique among vases. It was lined with a layer of glass inside its outer layer of glass so that there was an air space between the two transparent walls though the two segments were fused together at the top and at the base.

Well, every Good Friday that vase was the center of attention in the community. There wasn't a neighbor that would miss going to look at it, including young Victor Barger. It seems that on Good Friday morn the enclosed air space in the object would fill with blood and it would stay filled until Easter morning. Then slowly the red substance would diminish and disappear not to be seen again until the next Good Friday!

The old woman declared the blood was a token reminder of the Christ's sacrifice. Nobody was ever able to solve the mystery of what happened in that vase, lease of all any of Victor's family, who, to this day, can offer no solution.

In Berks County, Pennsylvania, lurks the pieces of a haunted bed. A woman bought the item a few years ago at a good bargain price from a couple who seemed, now that she looks back on it, most eager to make the sale. It wasn't long, says this lady before she realized why. The bed had a demon. She says she discovered that very shortly after bringing it home. She could feel its icy presence in bed with her in the night, its clammy touch setting her skin to prickling from sheer horror. She finally dismantled the bed as the only way she could conceive of to dismember, so to speak, the evil spirit. It might have worked. He's never bothered her since.

One more unusual "possessed possession" and a rather touching one, I feel, exists in Berks County. An old lady there passed away one Christmas Eve. Many of her things the family left untouched and one one particular item they were careful to preserve for it was their grandmother's favorite belonging — her rocking chair. She used to sit in it for hours at a time, passing peacefully the long hours of the day.

Then it happened. The following Christmas Eve after the grandmother's death, the empty chair commenced to rock. It rocked and rocked all the evening. By the next day it had stopped. It was still all the rest of the year and no one came to give it much thought until, once again, it was Christmas Eve and the old wooden chair began to go back and forth again. Back and forth as though some gentle invisible form were in it pressing it into action.

The family felt disturbed and at a loss to explain what was happening. They didn't believe in ghosts so there was only one thing to do: put the chair out of sight in the attic.

But come Christmas Eve once more, the rocker came back into mind. Was it in motion again? Of course, they had to peek. And there was the chair, alone in the dusky gloom, rocking away as before.

Ghosts are a forebearing lot, it would seem. They do not give up easily on the non-believers.

Maybe that's the way everyone wants it, even the non-believers.

Devil's Half Acre

No recounting of local ghost lore would be complete without including the tale of the Devil's Half Acre in Upper Bucks County.

Its very name stirs up little shivers of awe.

In the "Bucks County Historical Proceedings" you find it described as a spooky, swampy area (due to a leak in the canal) squeezed between the River Road and the Delaware Division Canal in Plumstead Township. Just drive from Lumberville up to Upper Black Eddy and you'll pass it by.

Today there is little evidence of either the swamp or the devil, but traces of the tale still hovers in the area. For over a century and a half that spot of land has been known to the local townspeople as the "Devil's Half Acre." Why?

The answer goes back to the early days in the county when a stone tavern stood there plying the hard-muscled canal-diggers and later, the tough-cored rivermen with whiskey. It was an illegal operation as the tavern was not licensed to sell liquor.

Adding to the "agin-the-law-operations" was the resultant effect on the canal and river men. They spent the nights drinking, wenching and fighting each other until there was scarcely a townsperson who'd dare come within a stone's toss of the tavern after twilight.

In 1845 the stone tavern was bought by Stephen Durand, a member of the State Legislature. Under his ownership the structure took on its first respectability. The building itself was refurbished and a flower garden and fruit trees added to the surroundings. But after Durand's death, an aura of fright still clung to the place.

"It's the screams — the shrieking and hollering — you can hear after dark around the old place," maintained one oldtimer.

"Yep," added another, "that place ain't never gonna settle down. It was built on the Devil's doin's and it's gonna go on harborin' them for ever and a day!"

So the stories circulated about Bucks. "Those river boys ain't never goin' to be allowed to rest in heaven or hell. The Devil owns their souls and the very spot o' land where they lived with him, doin' his bidding!"

People walking the dark River Road at night declared they heard the raucous laughter and the wild shrieks of the Devil-owned river boys every time they passed by that parcel of land. Gradually the old stone home fell into decay. It was an "untouchable" in Bucks.

Today it stands restored by the river looking at its old historical face in the glassy waters. Its present owners are Mr. and Mrs. Donald Pollard.

Does their home catch the memory of heavy-booted canal men? Hear the cries of celebrating rivermen ringing through the trees after dark?

If so, it recalls those days and the ghostly tales alone.

Today, few remember that piece of land and its name.